BLACKPOOL
& THE FYLDE COAST
MEMORIES

The publishers would like to thank the following companies for their support in the production of this book

Ai Claims Solutions

Arnold School

Banks Carrington & Co.

Beaverbrooks the Jewellers

Burton's Foods

Clifton Quality Meats Ltd

Fox Brothers

Fylde Floor Co. Ltd

Lyndene Hotel

Partingtons Holiday Centres

First published in Great Britain by True North Books Limited
England HX3 6AE
01422 344344

ISBN 978 - 1906649104

Text, design and origination by True North Books
Printed and bound by The Amadeus Press

BLACKPOOL

& THE FYLDE COAST
MEMORIES

CONTENTS

INTRODUCTION

Everybody knows that Blackpool is Britain's top seaside resort. It has headed its league for over a century and has had few rivals in that time. Yet, although the town is justly proud of its proms and piers, its lights and laughter, its sands and shows, it has more than that to offer visitors and residents alike. Blackpool provides centres for educational and political conferences. It also has busy and thriving retail centres in the heart of town and in the dedicated areas for shopping on the outskirts. Manufacturing provides employment for locals in biscuit making and the government's National Savings and Investments centre at Marton provides work for many local employees. Although the main focus of this book is centred around Blackpool, the Fylde includes a delightful mix of towns, with Cleveleys and Fleetwood to the north and Lytham St Annes to the south, with Thornton and Poulton-Le-Fylde not far inland. Include smaller villages such as, Freckleton, Great Eccleston, Knott End and Wrea Green and you have a diverse mix. This is reflected within the pages of 'Blackpool & the Fylde Coast Memories'. However, the book makes no excuses for concentrating on the nostalgia with which we can all identify when we think back over the times we have been through in our own lives and allow ourselves to imagine what life was once like. The photographs and accompanying captions help take the reader back to the days when great grandpa was a lad and get a feel for what made the Fylde, its inhabitants and visitors, tick in days of yore.

Not everyone agrees that Blackpool got its name because an old drainage channel ran through here across a peat bog, discharging distinctive dark coloured water into the Irish Sea, but it is as good a reason as any. What is certain is that the town's name was on all the nation's lips by the mid-Victorian era. In medieval times, it was just a collection of farmsteads along the Fylde coast, but the 18th century interest in the medicinal properties of sea and spa bathing brought the first tourists to the area. In the 1780s, wealthy families built a private road into what would become the township. A regular stagecoach service with Halifax and Manchester was established and several hotels were built to offer hospitality to visitors to the Fylde. Henry Banks, later to be known as 'the father of Blackpool', bought land at Lane Ends in 1819 and built the first holiday cottages. The coming of the railway in 1846 accelerated the rise to prominence as a resort. Consequently, more holiday accommodation was built and entertainment centres established. Millworkers from the Lancashire cotton towns flooded to the coast during their Wakes Weeks and the early provision of electricity on a widespread scale helped advance the town's reputation even more. It was the world's first municipality to have electric street lighting and had its own electric tram service over 15 years before London instituted its service.

The companies and organisations which have developed and thrived in the town over recent decades are many. We take pleasure in including in this book histories of an outstanding selection of different companies whose contribution to the development and sustainability of the town's economic prosperity is a matter of record. With their co-operation and access to their respective photographic archives, we have been able to tell their stories and hopefully trigger the memories of local people who have worked for them or been touched by their part in community life.

Now has come the time to enter that world of nostalgia we mentioned earlier. Return to days when you could stroll along Abingdon Street, window shopping for a new frock at Wilcock's outfitters, or take tea at Lockhart's Café at the junction of Adelaide Street and Bank Hey Street. Get into the mood by turning on the wireless and tuning into the Light Programme to listen to that adopted son of Blackpool, Jimmy Clitheroe, telling you that 'I'm all there with me cough drops'. Pop a Fisherman's Friend into your mouth and close your eyes and imagine you are at Wembley back in 1953 when Matthews crossed for Perry to notch that fourth decisive goal. As Dean Martin put it, 'Memories are made of this'.

TEXT	ANDREW MITCHELL, STEVE AINSWORTH
PHOTOGRAPH COMPILATION	TONY LAX
DESIGNER	SEAMUS MOLLOY
BUSINESS DEVELOPMENT EDITOR	PETER PREST

VICTORIAN & EDWARDIAN
BLACKPOOL

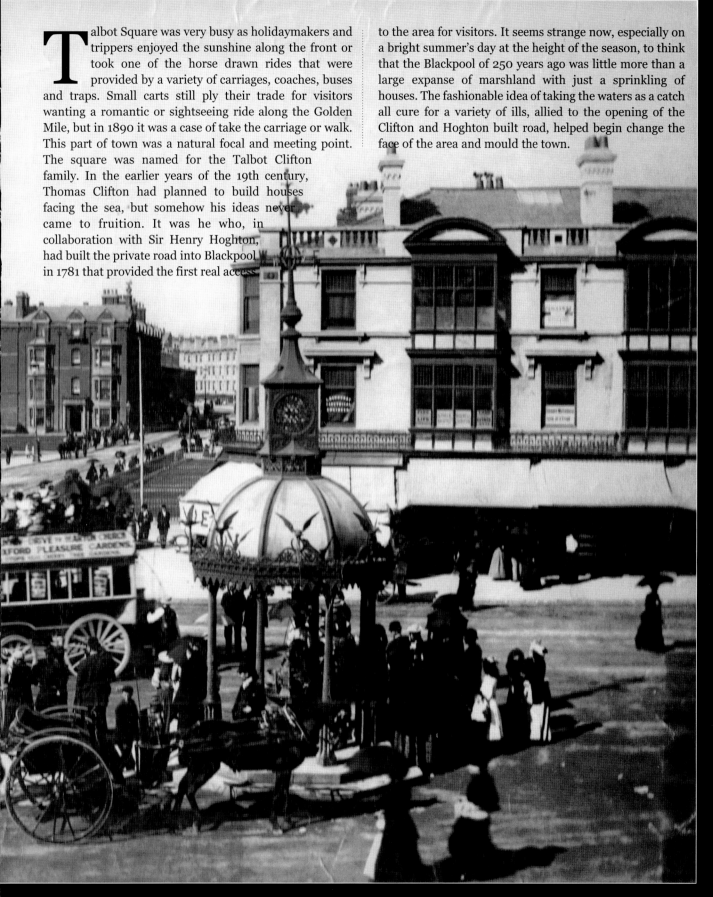

Talbot Square was very busy as holidaymakers and trippers enjoyed the sunshine along the front or took one of the horse drawn rides that were provided by a variety of carriages, coaches, buses and traps. Small carts still ply their trade for visitors wanting a romantic or sightseeing ride along the Golden Mile, but in 1890 it was a case of take the carriage or walk. This part of town was a natural focal and meeting point. The square was named for the Talbot Clifton family. In the earlier years of the 19th century, Thomas Clifton had planned to build houses facing the sea, but somehow his ideas never came to fruition. It was he who, in collaboration with Sir Henry Hoghton, had built the private road into Blackpool in 1781 that provided the first real access

to the area for visitors. It seems strange now, especially on a bright summer's day at the height of the season, to think that the Blackpool of 250 years ago was little more than a large expanse of marshland with just a sprinkling of houses. The fashionable idea of taking the waters as a catch all cure for a variety of ills, allied to the opening of the Clifton and Hoghton built road, helped begin change the face of the area and mould the town.

The Palatine Hotel stood on the corner of Houndshill, opposite Central Station at the end of Adelaide Street. With a name evocative of the home of a Roman emperor, this prestigious hotel was one of Blackpool's finest. Equipped with sea water baths for those wishing to partake of the curative powers of salt, the Palatine was also one of the first to be able to boast that it was lit by electricity and could offer hot and cold running water. Prior to the coming of the Palatine, a row of houses stood on Queen's Terrace. They were demolished in 1848 and eventually replaced by this grand edifice that also boasted of serving the finest cuisine in the area. Sadly, the Palatine was demolished in 1973, along with the New Inn, and replaced by shops and amusements.

Top right: Read's Saltwater Swimming Baths offered a pleasant dip that also had therapeutic benefits, if you took notice of the claims that were made on behalf of the stuff that goes to make up the Irish Sea. In years to come, casting an eye at the murky mess that lapped our shores might have made you think twice about risking so much as a big toe into something that became little better than an open sewer. Fortunately, for both the sake of our health and the reputation of Britain's beaches, various Acts of Parliament and local initiatives helped make sea bathing a pleasurable and relatively safe experience once more. Read's Baths were situated on South Beach. The sexes were segregated, of course, as Victorians would have nothing to do with anything that might inflame the passions. The idea of swimming close to a member of the opposite sex or seeing someone in a one piece, all covering costume was just too racy to be contemplated. The men used a bath that was 60 feet in length and 24 feet in width. A daily supply of 60,000 gallons of pure, tepid, filtered seawater was needed to keep it topped up. Ladies had a slightly smaller pool, measuring 40 feet by 15 feet. A husband and wife could gain admission for the joint price of a shilling (5p), but had to swim apart. Those too embarrassed or too proud to splash in the briny with others could avail themselves of small, private baths. Indicating how status conscious our forefathers were, even these were rated as first or second class baths and charged accordingly at one shilling or nine pence (4p). Jonathan Read opened his facility in 1861 and was a man with an eye for an opening. As well as the baths, he built a market and bazaar at the back so that he could maximise the profit to be made from the site.

Although the face of Abingdon Street has changed radically since 1888, when this scene was captured, it is recognisable because of the two major buildings that still dominate the skyline today. A modern photographer would have the 120 foot high dome of the Winter Gardens in his viewfinder, with the tower of the parish church looming high above the shops that presently surround it on the edge of Cedar Square and Church Street. The original St John's, or St John the Evangelist to give its true title, was consecrated by the Bishop of Chester on 6 July 1821. This modest building was soon found to be too small to accommodate a rapidly growing town and within a decade it had to be enlarged. Even so, it still could not cater for the rising numbers who wished to participate in its services. The 19th century was a period when all and sundry attended church as a matter of course. In 1875 work began on a replacement church. This time, the Bishop of Manchester conducted the consecration of the new church. On 25 June 1878, some 1,223 people, including Blackpool's first Mayor, Dr W H Cocker, were present at the ceremony.

Left: In 1891 the foundation stone was laid marking the moment that work began on the tower that would become the iconic symbol of Blackpool as a place of touristic pilgrimage. As the first elements of the structure were put in place and it started to take shape above the buildings below, most people were not completely sure how the finished product would look. They need not have worried. The architects Maxwell and Tuke, with advice from consultant engineer RJG Read, had things well in hand. The work was tendered out to the Worcester firm of Heenan and Froude. William Froude was one of the great Victorians and it was he who invented the hydraulic dynamometer in 1877. The company is still alive and well today, trading as Froude Hofmann. The idea for a tower to boost Blackpool's standing came from a visit Mayor John Bickerstaffe made to Paris in 1899 to view the Great Exhibition. He was impressed by the newly opened Eiffel Tower. This was to be the world's tallest structure until New York's Chrysler Building opened in 1930. Although our tower was only to be about half the height of the Parisian one, Bickerstaffe was keen for Blackpool to boast a tower that would have something in common with the chic French. It opened on 31 May 1894 and over 3,000 customers paid the sixpence admission fee.

Above: The 1890 view across the shore towards Central Promenade shows how reliant we once were on the horse on land and the sail at sea. The two combined quite neatly in the example of the boat cart that carried passengers from the sea front to the boats waiting to ferry them on a jaunt around the bay or on a longer excursion further down the coast or even across to the Isle of Man. The owner of the sailboat to the left was someone who obviously had an eye for maximising profit as the canvas on his vessel was used to advertise a cure for what Victorians called 'the rheumatics'.

Left: As the 19th century drew to a close, Blackpool's prominence as a leading resort continued to grow. It already boasted a pair of handsome piers, but this was still not enough. There was an increasing demand for a music and social centre that could outshine what was on offer at North Pier. The South Pier Jetty Company was formed and subscription levels soon reached £50,000. Victoria Pier, as it was originally christened, was built by the Leeds Stanningley Ironworks of J Butler and Company in 1892-3. The 429 foot pier had room for 36 shops, a bandstand and shelters. The Grand Pavilion was erected by J D Harker and was designed to accommodate up to 3,000 people. Various alterations in the early 20th century were carried out when the promenade was widened and again in 1918 with the opening of the Victoria Cinema. More modification took place in 1938 when South Pier, as it became more commonly known, was widened by 20 feet and the 1,300 place Regal Pavilion built. H H Vickers and Son drove reinforced concrete piles some 40 feet into the sands to provide extra strength and stability. The pier was badly hit by major fires in 1958 and 1964 that saw the destruction of the Grand Pavilion and Rainbow Theatre. Rebuilding after the second fire helped change its face to one of a more modern amusement and entertainment centre.

In 1780, there were just about 50 houses in the vicinity served by simple, dusty roads. However, entrepreneurs recognised that the Georgian interest in the curative properties of seawater, allied to the growing fashion among the well-to-do for holidaying at the coast, meant that there was what would now be called a niche in the marketplace. The hotel trade started to take off. More modest establishments charged 10d (4p) per room, but Lawrence Bailey decided that he could make more than that. He built his hotel in 1785 and ensured that it was superior in fittings to any of his rivals. This meant that he could also charge a more princely amount for rooms in Bailey's. He charged 3s 4d ((17p) per night, with an additional 1s (5p) for dinner and a further 8d (3p) for breakfast. The total cost of bed, breakfast and evening meal came to 5s (25p). This was about the average weekly wage for a labourer, so you had to be worth quite a bit to afford Bailey's prices. It was replaced by the Metropole in the late 1860s. It still boasts an exclusive location today, being the only hotel in the town to enjoy a position on the promenade. Its uninterrupted views have ensured a place in the premier league of hotels that dates back almost one and a half centuries. Pictured c1900, many of the hotel residents availed themselves of the use of the bathing huts on the beach below.

Above: The Tower was a new attraction in August 1895, having been completed just a year earlier. The motorcar was almost unheard of and Victorians enjoyed the stroll along the promenade, even if the world and his wife seemed to be out and about on that summer's day. Note how people came out dressed in their finery. This was a special occasion and to be seen out and improperly dressed was not an option.

Left: Taken around 1900, this view of Blackpool Tower, built by Maxwell and Tuke, was taken looking north along the sea front. To the right is the Great Wheel or Big Wheel that was located at the Winter Gardens. Large crowds can be seen enjoying the sea breezes as they head along the promenade. Movable bathing huts were positioned along the slipway, affording their occupants a degree of decency and modesty as they prepared to take to the water. Some of the huts offset their cost by having advertisements for the likes of Beecham's Pills inscribed on their coachwork.

Left: Close to the Central Promenade, these ladies and the child look somewhat overdressed for a donkey ride. Their clothing was a far cry from the bikinis, thongs and miniscule bits of material that would be called bathing costumes a century later. In 1903, you covered up whatever the temperature. With tightly laced corsets underneath the voluminous black garb, it is little wonder that such women were prone to swoons and fainting fits.

Before we poke too much fun at the ladies, have a look at the men. While they would not need strapping into their undergarments, they still wore several more layers than was really necessary. Surely a bowler hat was just a touch too much, or so you might think. What price the poor nipper in the foreground? This little love was hardly equipped for a day scrabbling in the sand, building castles, or ferreting around in some seaside pool, keeping an eye out for the occasional crab. For this group, entertainment was a serious business and it would seem that the word 'fun' was not in their vocabulary.

Above: Along at the Pleasure Beach is a stall called 'Arabian Derby' where punters can take part in a camel race that unfolds before their eyes in a scene that is reminiscent of the old table top horse racing game, 'Escalado'. But, these riders were experiencing the real thing. We suppose it made a change from donkeys. You might have imagined this happening at some later stage in Blackpool Zoo, but on the sands? Well, I never.

Left: The photograph of Imperial Crescent on North Promenade, taken in c1905, includes a view of Park Hotel on the right. It opened as the Royal Edward in the 1840s, later becoming the Claremont Hotel when only the two right hand bays were in existence. It was renamed as the Carlton Hotel in the 1920s and a sun lounge extension was added in 1937. The road to the right leads to Dickson Road and Pleasant Street.

Below: Hiram Maxim's Flying Machine was built in 1904 and is still going strong today. Seen in the year after it opened, this attraction has stood the test of time and come out well on top. With over a century of service, it must be one of the most enduring rides ever constructed. The inventor was born in America in 1840 and is best remembered across the globe for the machine gun he developed. A born tinkerer with things, he was involved in attempts to produce such varied items as the first lightbulb and aeroplane, though failed to lead the way in either field. He was more successful in his military exploits. He emigrated to Britain in 1881 and became a naturalised citizen in 1899. By then he had perfected the machine gun used as standard by the British Army for many years. Maxim was knighted for his work in 1901 in one of the last ceremonies performed by Queen Victoria before her death. His Flying Machine fairground ride was a source of funding for some of his other less successful work. The first example was unveiled at the Earls Court Exhibition and copies were soon installed at Crystal Palace, Southport and Brighton, as well as Blackpool where the entrance to the ride today still bears its full name, 'Sir Hiram Maxim's Captive Flying Machine'. As well as his gun, Maxim also invented a device to capture and kill mice, better known as the mousetrap.

Above: The photograph dates from Edwardian times when Fleetwood was a bustling and thriving deep-sea fishing port. By the inter-war years, when the fishing industry was at its height, it employed some 9,000. The sea front along the north shore was developed in resort fashion, but with the aim of attracting visitors for whom the brashness of Blackpool was too daunting. The Marine Hall entertainment complex, the golf course and the impressive Model Yacht Pond and Club all date from this era. The first fully automated telephone exchange in Britain was opened on 15 July 1922. These developments lay in the future for Herbert Ramsey as he poked the sands with a stick, under the watchful eye of the women who were typically overdressed. It would be some years before they would feel confident enough to shed some of their clothing as well as their inhibitions. Behind them, we can make out the lifeboat house that was erected in 1897 and the Lower or Beach Lighthouse, designed by Denham and Burton and erected in 1840. The Bourne Arms Hotel, Knott End-on-Sea can be seen in the distance, across the River Wyre. The 'Prince of Wales' ferry was a 500 ton vessel, built on the Clyde and used on the service over the Irish Sea to Belfast. Ferries making the short journey across the river began running in the 1830s, powered by oar and sail. The first steam launch did not run until the mid 1890s.

Above: Bailey's Hotel was one of the first hotels to be built and helped herald the birth of Blackpool as a resort. Enlarged and extended, and now part of the Metropole, it still stands on the North Shore as an imposing link with those earlier times. This photograph shows happy tourists bathing, horse riding and playing cricket in the shadow of the famous hotel. The clothes may change, but the pursuit and delivery of pleasure and enjoyment continues today, just as it did all those years ago.

The British royal family was treated with a mixture of deference, respect and admiration in the early 20th century. Much of this regard was down to the way in which we regarded Queen Victoria, the longest reigning monarch we have had. The warm way we felt about her was transferred to her relatives, including Princess Louise. She was Victoria's granddaughter and sister of King George V. Louise became the Princess Royal in 1905 and a significant figure in official circles. On 2 May 1912, she presided at the official ceremony held to open the static illuminations that marked the unveiling of a new section of the promenade. The Princess rode in a cavalcade, preceded by a marching band, and was cheered and feted the length of her journey. Locals respected her for attending as she had been widowed only a few months previously when her husband died of pleurisy, brought on by the after effects of being shipwrecked off the Egyptian coast.

The country entered a new, but shortlived, era in 1901 when Edward VII came to the throne. The Edwardian phase only lasted less than a decade as the new King was nearly 60 when he became our monarch. However, it heralded much change, especially on our streets. It saw the coming of trams and the development of motor cars. The bustling streets that were filled with shoppers, as here on Lytham Street in 1905, would soon echo to the clank of tramcars and the toots of the motor horn. It would drive a few to drink, but the Market Hotel on the left would cope with that well enough. The family on the left, just starting to cross the road, contrasts with the men

on the right. The latter have all the appearance of ordinary, working folk, with their flat caps and rough and ready clothing. The elegant women, the man under the boater and the kiddies dressed in their finery were a financial and social world apart. Some of the language used in the photograph is also from a different world. W Southworth was a 'boot factor'. It has been many a year since such a description of a trade appeared above one of our shops. Lytham Street is now known as Corporation Street.

ENTERTAINMENT, LEISURE & PASTIMES

The first Uncle Tom's Cabin was built high on the cliff tops near Bispham, 95 feet above the waves. Dating from around the mid 1850s, it was Blackpool's first house of entertainment. It took its name from the nickname given to Thomas Parkinson that in turn was based on the title of the popular novel by Harriet Beecher Stowe. The book that was published in 1852 outsold all the works of every other 19th century author, including Dickens, Scott, Stevenson, Austen, the Brontës and Twain. Even though it was an anti-slavery story, its theme touched the hearts of everyone in the English speaking world. Parkinson had large figures of three of the novel's characters made and he placed these for all to see on the roof of his own Uncle Tom's Cabin. The transatlantic link can be seen being continued in the older of the photographs, taken c1902, with its advertisement for 'American portraits'. As can be seen from the crowds who flocked there, the Cabin was a very popular attraction. Unfortunately, Mother Nature was too powerful for it. The constant battering of the waves on the headland caused gradual erosion. Bit by bit, lumps of rock fell into the sea and, before long, Uncle Tom's Cabin was facing a watery fate. The building was pulled down in late Edwardian times before it could topple over the edge. The present pub on Queen's Promenade that bears the same name was photographed in 1985. Although it can hardly be compared with the original, it has managed to perpetuate the name and provides modern visitors to North Shore with a jolly venue. The music by live bands and groups can be enjoyed, as can the attractive sights on display during heats for the title of Miss Blackpool.

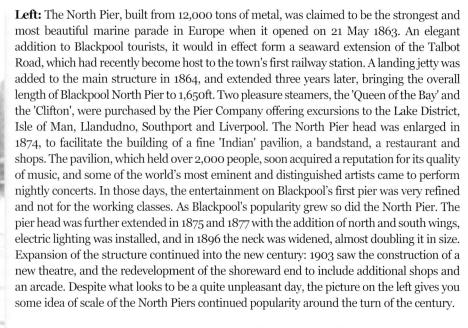

Left: The North Pier, built from 12,000 tons of metal, was claimed to be the strongest and most beautiful marine parade in Europe when it opened on 21 May 1863. An elegant addition to Blackpool tourists, it would in effect form a seaward extension of the Talbot Road, which had recently become host to the town's first railway station. A landing jetty was added to the main structure in 1864, and extended three years later, bringing the overall length of Blackpool North Pier to 1,650ft. Two pleasure steamers, the 'Queen of the Bay' and the 'Clifton', were purchased by the Pier Company offering excursions to the Lake District, Isle of Man, Llandudno, Southport and Liverpool. The North Pier head was enlarged in 1874, to facilitate the building of a fine 'Indian' pavilion, a bandstand, a restaurant and shops. The pavilion, which held over 2,000 people, soon acquired a reputation for its quality of music, and some of the world's most eminent and distinguished artists came to perform nightly concerts. In those days, the entertainment on Blackpool's first pier was very refined and not for the working classes. As Blackpool's popularity grew so did the North Pier. The pier head was further extended in 1875 and 1877 with the addition of north and south wings, electric lighting was installed, and in 1896 the neck was widened, almost doubling it in size. Expansion of the structure continued into the new century: 1903 saw the construction of a new theatre, and the redevelopment of the shoreward end to include additional shops and an arcade. Despite what looks to be a quite unpleasant day, the picture on the left gives you some idea of scale of the North Piers continued popularity around the turn of the century.

Below: The Winter Gardens boasted 'never a dull moment' and all the fun you wanted was available for just one shiny sixpence (2.5p). One small tanner, as the little coin was known, was still a significant amount in 1878 when the Gardens opened for the first time, but it bought an awful lot. Although primarily an indoor complex, it boasted an outdoor skating rink in its early days. One of Blackpool's most enduring and important attractions was built on the Bank Hey land owned by Dr W H Cocker, the town's first Mayor. Before the Winter Gardens Company was formed, he had shown an interest in developing entertainment centres. He bought the Prince of Wales Arcade in 1872, turning it into a menagerie and private aquarium. It was opened to the public four years later and part of the south wing of the aquarium survives today. The Prince of Wales Theatre opened nearby in 1877, with swimming baths being added in 1881. The Winter Gardens were given a makeover in the 1930s to bring them up to date. They now include several components that include the Opera House, the Pavilion Theatre, Empress Ballroom, Arena function room and Olympia exhibition hall. Such diverse events as the World Matchplay Darts Championship and major political party conventions are regularly held here.

Above: This is the sport of kings, along with a few members of the local gentry to make up the numbers. For a short while, Clifton Park Racecourse was one of the places to be seen if you wanted to get noticed in society. Many of the punters who attended a day's racing here were just as interested in the fashions and conversations as they were in the result of the 3.30. During the early 1900s, the land was used for flying carnivals when biplanes buzzed overhead. Racing on the ground rather than in the skies began when the track was formally opened on 1 August 1911. It seemed to be an immediate success as some 20,000 packed the course to watch the Coronation Cup. This race was named in honour of George V who had been crowned in Westminster Abbey just over a month earlier. Surprisingly, attendances started to fall off, but it was the outbreak of war in the summer of 1914 that ended its days as a race venue. In 1915, it was taken over by the Army and used as the King's Lancastrian Military Convalescent Home for injured servicemen. In addition to some permanent buildings, large tented wards were erected. The hospital continued in use until 1924 before being returned to serve the district's aviation needs as Squire's Gate. The airfield was used by small airlines in the 1930s, but was requisitioned by the government during World War II. Vickers built Wellington bombers here and flew them out of Stanley Park Aerodrome, now the site of Blackpool Zoo. In recent years, Blackpool International Airport, as the Squires Gate operation is now known, has seen some heady expansion.

Below: As well as portable gangways, boat carts were used to get trippers to and from the sailing boats waiting to take them on short excursions along the coast and around the bay. The lonely oyster stall was one of many shellfish outlets and other food stands that were dotted along the beach in days gone by. Oysters are now associated with high living, but they were once popular with the masses as they were a cheap and cheerful foodstuff, particularly in coastal areas and around the capital. Londoners, 200 years ago, were well served by large oyster beds off Whitstable and Colchester, among other centres. The molluscs were plentiful and a, thus affordable, source of nourishment. It was only with over harvesting in the 19th century that supply became limited. By the start of the last century, the oyster had become associated with wealth and privilege. There are no boat carts any more, but there are still boat cars running as trams. Shaped like a seagoing vessel, the first was introduced in 1933 by Walter Luff, the

network's controller. As well as being innovative in style, they were much safer for the conductor. He no longer had to make his way along the running board in order to collect fares as he did on the older Toastrack style of tram.

Right: Even before 'Come Dancing' was first broadcast in 1949, couples needed no excuse to take to the floor. They did not need the stimulus of the goggle box, but were doing what came naturally when taking a partner of the opposite sex into their arms. Of course, if a handsome beau was not available, it was acceptable to dance with another girl, though two men quickstepping together was not to be applauded. Joyce Grenfell's song, 'Stately as a galleon', about two matronly figures dancing 'bust to bust' was as far as single sex cavorting was allowed to go. Certain niceties had to be observed. As can be seen in the photograph, the man kept his hat on and the lady in the foreground kept her purse firmly within her grasp. Although some of the more exotic dances, such as the samba or bossanova, were not in our repertoire, every normal adult could manage a neat foxtrot or waltz. Being able to dance was like riding a bike in that the skill stayed with you forever.

Bottom: Ballroom dancing has made a comeback in recent years, largely thanks to BBC television coverage in its celebrity 'Strictly Come Dancing' competition. At one time, everybody at least knew how to waltz, quickstep and foxtrot. For the slightly more daring we could also manage a passable cha-cha-cha and rumba, though the samba was a bit too much for most of us to handle. Learning the basic turn, glide and chassis was essential in the courting game. No lad with two left feet was ever going to get a pretty girl to take his arm. Similarly, any lass who could not fishtail her way along the floor during the quickstep was destined for wallflower status. Dancing was also a necessary social skill. Heaven help the young executive who trod on the toes of the boss's wife at the annual dinner dance. Promotion was definitely put on hold for such a clumsy clod. The Winter Gardens' Empress Ballroom opened in 1896. With a floor area of 12,500 square feet, it was one of the largest in the world. With the decline in interest in ballroom dancing in the 1970s, part of the floor space was adapted for other uses, though it continued to host the Dance Festival that was first held in 1920. Now that TV has put dancing with a partner back on the map, perhaps we can hope for a revival in the fortunes of the Empress.

Right: Bank holiday fun riding the Big Dipper at the Pleasure Beach in Blackpool in 1953. The Big Dipper was first built in 1923 using John Miller's undertrack friction wheels, a safety feature which allowed designer and engineer to incorporate steeper exciting runs with more severe bends. The ride was an instant hit with Blackpool tourists at the time. Although the ride has grown over the years we have all experienced the timeless trepidation, as the train carriages click, click, click their way to the summit of the lift hill and then suddenly you are over the top and hurtling downwards at over 30 miles an hour. Great fun, but then there is always someone who wants to take things even further. In June 2000, Richard Rodriguez set the record for the longest round-the-clock endurance record, when he spent 2,000 hours (90 consecutive days and nights) on the Big Dipper in Blackpool. Of Richard's 17 records around the world, six of these were at the Pleasure Beach on the Big Dipper, the first of which was set in 1979.

Below: Some are amused, others intrigued, but the man with the briar firmly clenched in his teeth takes a fairly stoical view. The visitors to Olympia Palace were watching a performance taking place in one of the slot machines. Insert a humble penny and the Laughing Policeman burst into life. For about 30 seconds, a caricature, motorised plastercast figure of a bobby leapt about in a glass booth with the sound of hysterical and inane laughter echoing around the place. The attraction was inspired by variety artist Charles Jolly, the stage name of Charles Penrose. He recorded the song 'The Laughing Policeman' in 1922 and it was a surprising hit and became an integral part of his stage act up to his death in 1952. The song continued to be aired in radio record request shows, notably 'Children's Favourites' and 'Family Favourites', into the 1970s. Most people fall into two diverse camps when discussing this song. They either love it or cannot stand it. Perhaps the best comment that can be made is that Timmy Mallett recorded it in the 1990s.

Right: The travelling entertainers who set up their Punch and Judy stalls on beach fronts and fairground sites were only too happy to label themselves as 'professors'. Although Professor J Green's booth had been going since 1880, the history of the hook nosed little man who beats his wife, has a go at a bobby and is gobbled up by a crocodile dates back much further. He was even mentioned in a diary entry Samuel Pepys made for 9 May, 1662. However, most people trace him a little further back than that to the Italian character Pulcinells or Punchinello who was first seen in the 16th century. In the early days of the show in Britain, the Punch and Judy story was performed by marionettes, sometimes in theatres or taverns, but usually at fairs and the like. As this form of entertainment was expensive to support and the equipment cumbersome to move around the country from one showground to another, the show had evolved into a puppet told story in an appropriately sized booth. Additionally, from about 1800 onwards the target audience became younger and younger. Initially, the content was much more satirical and bawdy, but this was toned

down as it became evident that children were now the focus. By Victorian times, the Punch and Judy show was very much as we know it today. This group of fascinated kiddies were on Blackpool sands in the early 1930s. They were not traumatised by the violence; they just laughed themselves silly and shouted themselves hoarse.

Left: In this postwar photograph we get the impression that the sun was shining brightly as quite a few of the kiddies have screwed up their eyes or shaded them with a hand or arm. They were watching a Punch and Judy show. Most of the children look somewhat bemused and one or two a tad worried. No doubt Mr Punch has just laid into his wife and instructed the audience 'That's the way to do it'. Of course, you seldom see such a show on the beach any more as the humour of the show does not sit well with the politically correct fraternity.

Below: It was warm work being one of General Booth's followers, especially if you were of the fairer sex. On a bright summer's day, when nearly everyone else was flat out in the sunshine, the women from the Salvation Army had to appear in their modest uniform, bonnets firmly in place. Perhaps it is just nostalgia talking, but it did seem that back then we had summers that were worthy of the name. In 1947, Edrich and Compton revelled under the blue skies and knocked up more runs on the cricket field than had been seen before or have been since. The choice of hymn sheet matched the weather. The children's beach mission included a rendition of 'All things bright and beautiful' and it is a little surprising that the words had to be displayed. This most popular of songs would surely have been part of every kiddies' Sunday School repertoire, but perhaps the 'Sally Army' was playing safe. As time went by, this religious group gained greater acceptance and came to be regarded with affection. It was not always the case. Founded in 1865 by William and Catherine Booth as the East London Christian Mission, this evangelical organisation was vociferous in its opposition to the use of alcohol. This did not sit kindly with large numbers of the working classes who objected at the dictatorial stance being taken against what they perceived as a simple pleasure. Salvation Army meetings were often broken up by gangs of ne'er-do-wells throwing bricks and even rats. However, time is a healer and the Army became more accepted and respected when it was seen to be actively assisting the poor and underprivileged. By the time these soldiers of the Lord appeared on Blackpool beach, even hardened boozers in the roughest of public bars stopped swearing long enough to buy a copy of the 'War Cry' when a bonneted young woman entered that normally men only sanctuary.

background, two young girls headed out towards the waves, all ready to practise their latest swimming stroke, possibly the doggy paddle. The bathing caps they wore were essential swimming uniform at the time. The rubberised or latex contraptions were quite strange pieces of apparel as they were awkward to stretch over a girl's hair and difficult to remove later when they seemed to be stuck to the head by seawater. The caps became particularly popular with women wishing to protect the permanent waves in their hair. Brightly decorated hats, with flowery motifs, colourful petals and the like, came into vogue in the 1950s. However, by the 1970s they had become outdated. Rather quaintly, when many men started wearing their hair at shoulder length in the late 1960s and early 1970s, some swimming baths brought in a rule banning them unless they wore caps.

Above: Those of us who were baby boomers and first saw the light of day at the end of the last war or just after it can recall our dads rolling up their trouser legs and our mums hitching up their skirts to enjoy the waves lapping around their ankles. Why is it that we cannot recall them ever getting into trunks or swimsuits? As children we swam and splashed happily, wearing next to nothing, but our parents always seemed fully clothed. These kiddies merrily leapt from a boat trailer into the waters, but many of the adults only risked the odd toe.

Right: This is dad taking care of the children in the middle of the last century. From his body language you can tell that he is having a whale of a time. It is not a case of wish you were here but more of wish I were somewhere else. The children had spent their pocket money on a couple of little boats and it was important that they kept their eyes on their new toys. There would be tears before bedtime if the sailing vessels got washed out to sea. In the

Above: These young women were having real fun in the mid 1930s. Their position in society and the roles that they now played were a long way removed from those experienced by their mothers. The right for all women to do something as simple as vote in an election had only been forthcoming in the late 1920s. It was still difficult for them to gain full acceptance in the workplace, but many men grudgingly accepted the position of those who had kept the country's factories and farms going during the 1914-18 War when so many were away at the front. Women no longer accepted their position as second class citizens. They threw off the yoke with which men had restrained them and they also abandoned the old, dowdy fashions that restricted freedom both of movement and spirit. In the 1920s, black, floor length dresses were discarded in favour of the short skirts and bright tops of the flapper generation. On Blackpool beach, these lovelies laughed at the thought of their grandparents' bathing machines and ankle length costumes. They romped across the sands in daring designs that showed acres of flesh and shocked the conservative element. The women also embraced the League for Health and Beauty. This organisation was founded in 1930 by Mary Bagot Stack with the aim of giving women the opportunity

The Pleasure Beach's first casino was built in 1913 in the style of a wedding cake. It was developed after World War I to include a restaurant, billiard room and theatre, but was demolished in 1937, with some difficulty as its reinforced concrete structure proved resilient to the initial attempts of those empowered to scrap it. The more modernist style of its replacement, designed by Joseph Emberton, was officially opened in May 1939. The architect was well known at the time for his up-to-date style, having represented Britain in New York in 1932 at the International Exhibition of Modern Architecture. Lord Stamp, president of the London Midland Scottish Railway presided at the ceremony. The casino has later become known as the Horseshoe Showbar. The word actually means 'small house', but has connotations of something much grander. We think of Casino Royale or the Grand Casino at Monte Carlo whenever the word is mentioned. Roulette wheels and baccarat shoes, elegant women with diamond earrings and men in tuxedos are sights that are conjured up when just hearing the word. James Bond and Ian Fleming have a lot to answer for. This view along the promenade at South Shore shows the Lido to the left. It was taken just after the end of the last war, not long before Agent 007 was created in print.

to enjoy physical fitness via a series of programmed exercises. Before long, large groups of largely young women were to be seen swinging Indian clubs and performing leap frogs and physical jerks in organised displays.

Left: Little lads never grow up. They just become a bit bigger and dafter as the years roll by. These dads enjoyed speeding along in what were called go karts at the time, though they bear little resemblance to the style of machines that bear that name today. They hardly whizzed along the boards doing several laps of the track as the top speed was restricted to little more than about 10 mph, but they felt as if they were the Billy Cottons of their day, racing round Goodwood or Brooklands in souped up speedsters that roared off the banking at speeds of 80 mph and more. In the 1930s, even ordinary motoring was something of a novelty for the working man. It was hardly surprising that he would act out his fantasy at a fair or pleasure beach. Secretly, he muttered 'brrm, brrm' under his breath and did his best to outdrive his pals in the other karts. Sometimes these toy circuits were referred to as 'speedways', though the term became synonymous with two wheeled vehicles on cinder tracks and was seldom used for cars after the war. When the men had finished their allotted laps of the track they could be heard telling off their sons who had stumbled and cut their knees. 'Grow up, lad', a father would say. Mum said nothing, other than to compliment her hubby on his skill in driving a toy car.

Money was tight after the last war as the country entered a period of austerity that was to last for over a decade. Spending on leisure activities had to be watched carefully, so time spent at the Lido was a comparatively cheap way of filling an afternoon in a useful and enjoyable capacity. Once the admission fee had been handed over you could stay for hours on end. The Lido opened on 9 June 1923. In the picture on the left children were taking an exercise class in the early 1950s, with the distinctive roofline of the theatre on the South Pier forming an attractive backdrop. Somewhat fancifully, the open air baths were said to have been modelled on the Coliseum in Rome. Whatever the truth of the statement, the popularity of the baths was not in doubt. Over a million bathers and spectators passed through the turnstiles in the first two years. The terraces were often packed with sun worshippers and these were also used as catwalks by budding beauty queens in the contests that became very popular before the second world war. The Cotton Queen was one of the most popular of these events and crowds flocked to see representatives of about 20 local towns, including Nelson, Chorley and Middleton, parading in front of them. There was no suggestion that such contests were demeaning to women. In fact, the majority of the spectators was female. The Lido even made it into the movies when it was featured in the 1934 Gracie Fields' film, 'Sing as we go'. Sadly, a piece of Blackpool history was lost when it was demolished in February 1983 after 60 years' service. The site was redeveloped as a leisure centre said to resemble a giant sandcastle.

Right: Divinity and religion were not the sort of things to attract punters to visit the various booths and sideshows at Blackpool Olympia just before the last war. The public wanted mysticism and magic instead. It was even better if that world of mystery came from overseas. We had a patronising view of anything east of Calais, especially if it came from even further away and beyond Europe. There was even a geography book in some primary schools entitled 'People from strange lands'. Just think how the politically correct educationalists of today would view such a tome. Apoplexy would be

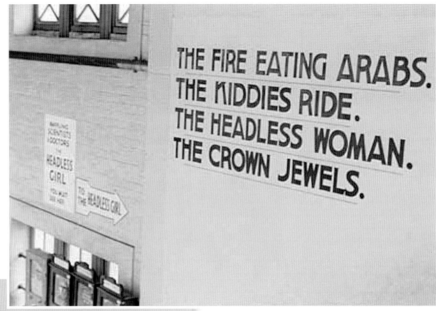

THE FIRE EATING ARABS.
THE KIDDIES RIDE.
THE HEADLESS WOMAN.
THE CROWN JEWELS.

rife. Fire eaters were a commonplace entertainment. They had been around in circuses, at fairs and on the music hall stage for donkeys' years. But, include Arab in the headline and you had a different act. Now there was something a little bit more interesting than Fred Higginbotham from Padiham waving burning sticks about. The headless woman was also that little bit special. Of course, any headless woman is remarkable, but this one was Chinese. She was guillotined to a mixture of shock and scepticism in the audience, but her nationality made it all more of a spectacle. She was just that little bit more entertaining than the bearded lady from Southport or the five legged cow from Ainsdale.

Left: The Crown Jewels were on display in Olympia Palace in 1938. Needless to say, they were not the ones that Colonel Thomas Blood attempted to pinch from the Tower, of London that is and not Blackpool, back in 1671. However, even though holidaymakers knew that they were going to be conned out of their threepence, they took it in good part. That was part of the game they played with the proprietors. The more outlandish the claim, the better the trick and the enjoyment of the spoof was all the greater for it. This façade can still be seen at the corner of Coronation Street and Adelaide Street, though the cupola has disappeared. Olympia Market is now to the left of this part of the Winter

Gardens. The Olympia exhibition and amusement hall was added in 1928, being built on the site where the 1896 Great Wheel once stood. The building is often used today as a banqueting suite, conference centre or trade exhibition hall. With 2,600 square metres of floor space, its dimensions are quite impressive. It is not surprising that it was once home to dozens of booths, funfair stalls and slot machines. As a fun palace, the Olympia was one of the best sources of entertainment in the days when our pleasures were much simpler and easier to be catered for.

Above: You can trace the success of girl groups from Girls Aloud to Bananarama and then on to the Supremes, Ronettes and Crystals. Before them, we listened to the Kaye Sisters, the Andrews Sisters and the Boswell Sisters. But, lasting longer than any of them is a trio of girls from Bethnal Green in London. They hold the record for longevity for a singing group in performing with an unchanged line up for 60 years. The Beverley Sisters are an essential part of the history of British light entertainment and popular music. They were born as the Chinery sisters, but took the stage name Beverley at the start of their careers. Jocelyn (Joy) was born in 1929 and twins Babette (Babs) and Hazel (Teddy) in 1932. They were the daughters of an established music hall double act, Coram and Miles, so the stage was in their blood. They began performing together professionally in the late 1940s and were seen as Britain's answer to the Andrews Sisters, a top wartime American trio. The Beverley Sisters' stock rose dramatically during the 1950s when they proved to be photogenic and television became almost a second home for them as they guested on numerous shows. They only had a handful of hit records, including 'Sisters', 'I saw mommy kissing Santa Claus' and 'Little Drummer Boy', but their stage shows and summer seasons were always sold out. Joy married England soccer captain Billy Wright in 1958. Here they were opening the £300,000 Savoy Bowl as they rolled the first strike on 17 December 1963.

Below: Blonde model and Marilyn Monroe look-alike, Miss Lesley Langley, of Bayswater, London, strides out purposefully in front of an enthusiastic crowd in Blackpool. Miss Langley had just been elected as Miss United Kingdom in September 1965, winning 1st Prize of 1,000 guineas, plus £150 to buy a wardrobe for the Miss World Contest. She would be lucky to get a decent bathing 'cossy' for that money these days never mind a full wardrobe!

Right: Blackpool has for a long time been associated with all things beautiful. These gorgeous and shapely young ladies epitomise the bathing beauty era. The picture, at the South Shore Open Air Baths, dates from 1959 and features a clearly delighted winner of the Miss Blackpool contest, along with the two runners up. The lucky man in the picture was no less than Edmund Hockeridge, the bass-baritone crooner, who was a judge in the contest The good looking vocalist enjoyed phenomenal success in the 50s and 60'

in the ring were 'The British Bulldog' and the 'Blackpool Rock', which originated from the fact that prior to boxing he used to work in the Blackpool Rock factory. It was also to do with his rugged, no nonsense fighting style and after turning pro he won his first twelve bouts, eleven by knockout, until coming up against Henry Cooper in May 1956. He lost to Cooper three times in his career, although in one of the contests it seemed as though London had done enough to win the fight. Despite the first loss to Cooper, he would go on to win eight out of his next 10 fights. In 1958 he won the British and Commonwealth titles from Joe Erskine. Although he lost them the following year to Cooper, it did propel him to a world title shot four months later against Floyd Patterson in Indianapolis. After a valiant effort London was stopped in the eleventh round. A series of mixed results followed until he received a second shot at immortality with a world title fight against Muhammad Ali in August 1966. One of London's all time heroes, Ali gave a vintage performance to stop him in three rounds. He continued to fight world class opponents until he lost to rising star Joe Bugner in 1970. After retiring from boxing, London became a businessman in Blackpool, owning several nightclubs, and is still a fitness fanatic running 12 miles most days. Teetotal all of his life, in 2006 it was revealed that he was still only a few pounds over his fighting weight. He is also involved in raising funds for local charities and sporting needs in Blackpool.

The Miss World phenomenon was started by Eric Morley in 1951, when Swedish beauty Kerstin 'Kiki' Haakonson became the first to wear the crown. The BBC televised Miss World from 1959 to 1979 and Thames Television carried it from 1980 to 1988. At its peak the show drew in an audience of 27.5 million in Britain alone.

Right: British and Empire heavyweight champion Brian London (left), of Blackpool, and his Bellingham challenger Henry Cooper are pictured at 41 Great Windmill Street, in London, where they weighed in for their title fight at Earls Court in 1959.

Brian London, real name Brian Sydney Harper, was born on 19 June, 1934 in West Hartlepool but moved to Blackpool at the age of 16 and has lived there ever since. He had a successful amateur career losing only two fights before turning professional in 1955. His nicknames

OUT & ABOUT

Below: Indian mysticism, fakirs and the wonder of the east captivated the imagination of the British public in the interwar years in a way that it had not done before. Perhaps Gandhi and his constant appearances on newsreels and in the press had something to do with it. Maybe it was popular fiction, such as James Hilton's 'Lost Horizon' and its tale of the magical Shangri-La, or the last influences of the British Raj, but there is no doubting the fascination that was displayed. In one booth at Olympia, a very brown skinned man, with greying black hair, was a popular attraction for visitors to the Winter Gardens in 1938. Calling himself Sharma, he dressed in a loincloth and used a bundle of rags for a pillow as he lay down to rest. But his bed was no ordinary one as his had 4,000 nails for a mattress. Pop-eyed crowds, emitting appropriate oohs and aahs, leaned over the edges of the four foot deep pit where he lay. Sharma fingered a set of beads around his neck and seemed oblivious to those watching him, though he would have been only too aware of the admission price that had been paid. With frequent mention of Allah, a colleague by the name of Tajan lectured the spectators on such diverse matters as the wonders of holy men, yogis and mystics, plus the doings of exotic animals and reptiles. Elsewhere a snake charmer played a recorder-like instrument as a cobra raised its head from within a wicker box. All this was yours for just a few coppers.

Right: Looking east along Church Street, the crowds were out in force in 1951. Obviously, many people had money to spend, but in truth it was not a time of plenty. Although the war was some six years behind us, the economic havoc that it left behind was still with us. Rationing was still with us and the Labour government we voted into power in 1945 had brought us the benefits of the National Health Service but little other evidence that the country had gained from abandoning Mr Churchill and his allies. We were also running scared from the threat of communism and the influence of the Soviet Union elsewhere in the world. Some actually embraced the idea that democracy was to be abandoned in favour of handing over control to the state. The News Theatre on the left of the street offered little hope in its films of current events. Not many people had televisions, so moving pictures of news had to be seen via the cinemas. This one was part of a chain of dedicated movie houses. We learned that there was trouble on the other side of the world where the western world was being dragged into a conflict in Korea. Would we ever learn?

Above: The seafront sideshow that was packing them in the very late 1930s had its origins nearly a decade earlier. When the apparently dashing Army Captain, Leslie Barker, failed to appear at a bankruptcy court in 1929, it did not seem to be a story that was very newsworthy. However, it was to become one of the titillating scandals of the 1930s. A warrant for his arrest was issued and, on being apprehended, Barker was examined by a police doctor who announced that he was in fact a she. Barker's friends were surprised, but his wife, Elfrida, was astonished. They had been married for six years, but their lack of intimacy had been explained away as being due to wounds received in the 1914 War. Apparently, he/she had been born in 1895 as Lilias Irma Valerie Barker. She served as a nurse during the war, was briefly married to a soldier and had two children by another man. She reinvented herself and 'married' Elfrida in 1923. A trial was held at the Old Bailey and, not surprisingly, the general public was fascinated. Puzzled prosecutors decided to accuse her of two counts of perjury, relating to her marriage and claim of an Army rank. Lilias served nine months in Holloway and later sold her story to the Daily Mail. After drifting through a series of jobs following her release from prison, in 1937 she began a career as a sideshow attraction. Her time in Blackpool showed that people still remembered the salacious case as they queued out onto the street in order to get a glimpse. She died in 1960, by then calling herself Geoffrey Norton.

Below: After the last war, holidaymakers flooded back into the resort on the London and North Western Railway, anxious to recapture the carefree mood that Hitler had denied them over the previous six years. Guest houses were full again and landladies put up the No Vacancies cards in their bay windows once more. Visitors hoisted their cases on their shoulders and kiddies tucked their buckets and spades under their arms as they made their respective ways to their accommodation from Talbot Road Station. The railway came to Blackpool as early as 1846, giving the town a head start over many rivals. It was not long before visitors arrived in their droves, revelling in the freedom to travel long distances in a short time when compared with the dirty, dusty journey by road. Such was the volume of traffic that the station had to be completely rebuilt in 1898. By then, Blackpool was well established as Britain's major holiday destination. Talbot Road Station was demolished in 1974 and rebuilt once more, this time on the site of the former Queen Street excursion platforms, based on the 1938 concrete canopy. Sacred Heart Church, Talbot Road, was the first Catholic place of worship in the town. Its foundation stone was laid on 30 May 1856 and Mass was first celebrated here on 8 December 1857. It was here that local entertainer, Tony Melody, worshiped regularly up to his death in 2008.The church was designed by Edward Pugin, son of Augustus Pugin. The latter was one of the architects involved in the rebuilding of the Houses of Parliament. Edward was also involved in work on Shrewsbury Cathedral and Scarisbrick House.

Above: Two youngsters in bathing costumes wander towards the cameras in one of the little gardened areas along the front at Cleveleys as other holidaymakers walk the promenade more formally attired. The golden sands and the views over Morecambe Bay, across to the hills of the Lake District, and out towards the Isle of Man in the Irish Sea have brought visitors here on a regular basis since early Victorian times. Although the resort has its bingo halls, seaside entertainment, amusement arcades and main street shopping, it has kept its position as a more refined neighbour to that noisier place a little further to the south. In recent years, the seafront has undergone an expensive makeover, with a widened promenade, piazza and bandstand and improved walkway. The sea defences have been improved and Cleveleys is a place that is very much on the up. The sandy beach, where millions of castles have been built and swept away again on the tide, once provided the gravel that was used in the early 1800s to build a road to this part of the coast across Thornton Marsh.

Below: Victoria Road West cuts across the centre of the village as it runs from the

promenade over the A587 Fleetwood/Rossall Road to meet the A585 Amounderness Way at Anchorsholme. It was originally called Ramper Road, the name being derived from the ramparts or banks that enclosed the marshland there. The little tram stop, just visible on the left, is now situated quite prettily in the centre of a roundabout that helps traffic navigate around this spot. In the 1930s there was little need for such assistance as cars were still few and far between. People could stroll across the carriageway without too much worry. Unfortunately, some pedestrians mistook ease for carelessness with a result that this particular decade was the worst we have ever had for road accidents when comparing the volume of traffic with the numbers killed or injured. Cleveleys provides a buffer zone between the brashness of Blackpool and the more gentle tone of Fleetwood. In recent times it has benefited from being used by some as a place to which to retire and there are quite a few silver threads among the gold to be seen on any day of the week you care to visit. However, it was also well known to some of our forebears as a guide published in 1893 states that 'a small but increasing seaside resort midway between Fleetwood and Blackpool has become very popular in late years with business and professional gentlemen who are making it a residential resort.'

Below: This picture dates from the mid-1930s and features Lockhart's Café. The popular eating place was situated at the junction of Bank Hey Street and Adelaide Street, next door to Hill's Department Store, seen here whilst in the process of being extended. Sadly Hill's was destroyed in a major fire in the late 1960s.

Above: This was the area of Blackpool, in the age before car became king, where family holidays would begin and end. The grand canopied entrance to Blackpool Central Station is featured here on a Wake' Week afternoon in 1952. Here holiday makers would draw their first breath of fresh, Blackpool air as they arrived in the town before setting off to their guest house or hotel to unpack. Departing visitors would pause at the forecourt for one last look at Blackpool before returning to their home town. At the time this photograph was taken the train was the preferred method of travel for the majority of visitors to the town. Gradually, motorcars overtook rail transport and this sounded the death knell for the once frantically busy Central Station. Closure followed in 1964 and the land which once hummed with thousands of holiday makers on the busy platforms was turned over to car parking. The actual station building itself was put to use as a bingo hall, a sign of the times which lasted until the structure was pulled down in 1973.

Top right: Looking from Central Beach towards East Beach, the well known landmarks of the windmill and lifeboat station can be clearly made out in the distance. The first lifeboat station was based at Lytham in 1851, with another following at St Annes in 1881. This part of Britain has its own sad place in the annals of RNLI history. On 9 December 1886, three lifeboats from Lytham, St Annes and Southport answered a distress call from the 'Mexico', a German ship. Some 27 members of the service were lost in heavy seas as they attempted the rescue. The building is now a museum, not having seen active service since 1931 when a motor lifeboat was purchased and moored on the River Ribble. The windmill is also open to visitors, but fulfilled a working role when Richard Cookson leased a plot of land from the Clifton family and built what he described as a 'windy milne'. As the wealthy moved into the area and built substantial houses along this part of the coast, they railed against what they called an 'industrial nuisance'. Perhaps they were early members of the Nimby brigade, but the mill was there before their back yards had been laid out. A mini hurricane that swept across the front in 1919 caused the sails to rotate so quickly that sparks flew, quite literally, and the mill was destroyed by the ensuing fire. It was partly restored in 1921, but given a full makeover by the Council in 1989. The long stretch of green leading up to it is full of budding cricketers anxious to bowl out dad for a duck during the summer months.

Below: Clifton Street in Lytham runs parallel with Central Beach, close to the sea front. Garlick's the butcher, occupying a prime site on the left, was

typical of the period in Edwardian times when individual shops occupied their own particular niche in the food and provisions market. Ask a kiddie now where he would go to get meat, vegetables or bread and he will look at you as if you are daft. The butcher, greengrocer or baker are words they have only met via their modern history books. Before Sainsbury began the trend in Croydon in the middle of the last century, every High Street had its own specialist shops.

Housewives went along the row with their wicker baskets over their arms, often on a daily basis, selecting food for tea or the table the following day. It was stored in a cold larder as such luxuries as fridges were not commonplace until the late 1960s and beyond. The tramlines along Clifton Street were laid in the late 1890s. At one time, Lytham was quite novel in that it used gas powered trams. This street was named for the local squire, Thomas Clifton, and founder of Lytham Hall in the 1760s.

Above: This aerial shot of Fleetwood looks towards the docks and harbour and into the Wyre estuary. When Fleetwood pier was opened it was one of the last in the line of British piers that were built during the so called golden age of these structures in late Victorian and Edwardian days. It was some time in the development as a submission by Richard Edmunds was first made in 1892. A revised set of plans by GT Lumb was approved in 1909 and the pier opened on Whit Monday, 1910. Its 492 feet were largely intended to be used as a landing stage, with just a handful of amusements scattered along the decking. A pavilion was added in 1911. A small cinema was opened in 1942, but the most dramatic event occurred on 25 August 1952 when a

huge fire broke out that could be seen 20 miles away. It was rebuilt the following year and given a facelift in 1972, but could never compete with those at Blackpool. It closed in 2000, but was reborn once more three years later when new owners injected cash and life into the old attraction. The town's two major lighthouses are in the centre of the photograph.

Bottom left: A life on the ocean wave, or as near as you could get to it in the children's boating pool at Fleetwood without much though for health and safety. Many kiddies were allowed out on the water unaccompanied by an adult and without so much as a life vest for protection. Fun, fun, fun was the order of the day in an era when common sense rather than legislation was the byword. Fleetwood has also has its

successful Model Yacht Club, founded in 1929. The lake on Laidleys Walk, as we know it today, was opened in 1932. The official opening ceremony was performed by Earl Beatty, former Admiral of the Fleet and veteran of the Battle of Jutland, and a Tory MP for Peckham in the 1930s.

Below: There have been a few changes to Talbot Square since this picture was taken! The most dramatic change has been the removal of the odd-looking spire on the Town Hall building which was taken down in 1966 after concern was expressed about its ability to remain standing in high winds. Also gone since this picture was captured in the early 1950 is the elaborate bus and tram shelter which can be seen slightly left of centre of the image.

'kiss me quick' hats on show here. St Annes-on-Sea was undoubtedly a haven for the slightly older and more discearing holidaymaker of the 50s and 60s.

Above: The line of cars parked up along The Square, St Annes-on-Sea, almost echoes the sentiments of Henry Ford, that you could have one of his cars in any shade you wanted, as long as it was black. We did not worry too much about pretty hues and delicate pastel shades when the motoring boom hit these isles in the 1950s. All of a sudden, as the austerity years of the postwar period started to slip away, the ordinary man in the street became the one in the motor vehicle instead. Small family saloons were affordable, with the help of a little 'tick' and a friendly bank manager. Who cared if the colours were uniform? We had wheels, as they now say.

Below: A busy street scene appears to be from the mid-20th century along The Square, St Annes Road West, off Clifton Drive. Although only three miles from Blackpool this view gives off a much more open and peaceful atmosphere... no

Right: Situated on the promenade, sandwiched between Bonny Street and Chapel Street, Louis Tussaud's Waxworks has been one of the resort's attractions for many years. Louis was the great-grandson of Marie, the original Madame Tussaud who escaped the French Revolution and later came to Britain in 1802 and toured the country with her waxwork collection of famous figures of the day. She established a permanent site on Baker Street in London, so founding a dynasty of family exhibitions that continues to this day. Louis's collection takes up five floors and is constantly changing to reflect modern tastes. Popular five minute wonders come and go and are then melted down to help create the next transient celebrity to be honoured in effigy. Visitors can rub shoulders with pop stars and TV characters, as well as standing shoulder to shoulder with politicians and historical figures. Members of the royal family, sporting heroes and movie legends are all there for tourists to recognise and comment upon. The Chamber of Horrors is perhaps the most popular section. We just love to have a tingle run up our spines or that butterfly to begin fluttering in our stomachs. Consequently, murderers both real and fictional are the stars here. The Yorkshire Ripper ranks alongside Hannibal Lector and Count Dracula in this most blood curdling part of the exhibition. Better leave the landing light on tonight.

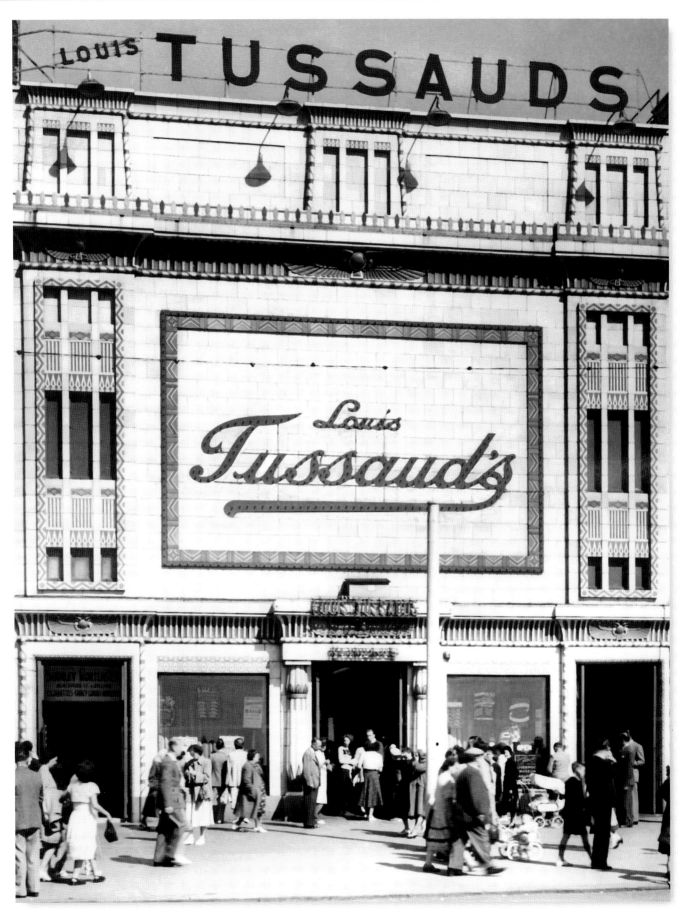

Above and below: Blackpool was no more than a handful of isolated farmsteads dotted along the coast at the time when farmers were bringing produce into important towns such as Preston and Kirkham. St John's Market needed merely the agreement of local businessmen, traders and minor officials in order to come into being. Taking its name from the nearby parish church, the market opened for business in 1844. It soon established a large clientele and was always a hubbub of noise and activity. Such was the demand for business and trade that the number of stalls was insufficient to deal with the demand.

In 1893, the market was extended from just Market Street to include an entrance from Lytham Street, later Corporation Street. As time went by, the building became outdated. It was replaced by the new market that opened on 28 May 1938 and the old one was demolished early the following January. British Home Stores now occupies the site. These views of St John's Market were taken about 80 years apart, but even the more modern of the two pictures of shopping styles looks out of place in the 21st century. Now it is all large malls and centres that have taken over our excursions into town in order to stock up on goods. Such places as the Houndshill Shopping Centre, with their associated multi storey car parks, are the current face of the retail trade.

Right and bottom right: The bathing belles and the strong man were part of the Blackpool Illuminations that lit up the sky in 1938. The setting of these lasses in such skimpy cozzies was quite a daring move for those in charge of selecting the tableaux during that era. But, Blackpool has never been a town to take a back seat when the word 'risqué' is on the agenda. Described as 'artificial sunshine', the light first shone on 18 September 1879 and consisted of just a dozen arc lamps that bathed the promenade in a bright glow. Now, they stretch from Bispham to Starr Gate and use over a million bulbs. The first

display that was akin to the modern one took place in 1912 to coincide with Princess Louise's visit when she officiated at the opening of the widened promenade. The illuminations were repeated in 1913, but mothballed during the Great War and not used again until 1925. The Chamber of Trade realised that the lights were a major tourist attraction. One of the highlights was the beautifully decorated and illuminated tram, crewed by men dressed as gondoliers. The first switch-on involving a major dignitary took place in 1934 when Lord Derby officiated. This was a significant year

for the town as 205 trains and 3,500 coaches brought passengers to see the attraction. Some 400,000 visitors passed along the promenade that weekend. The Tower was illuminated for the first time and 'the greatest free show on earth' really took off.

Above: 'Now then, pet. Do you remember that lovely Michael Fish doing the weather forecast this morning? He said something about sunny intervals, but I missed the bit about what came in between.' This flooding at South Shore is typical of the occasional reminder that the sea is a mighty force with which we have to reckon. As the beach level dropped because of erosion, the risk of flooding increased. In a major storm in 1927, huge chunks of the sea wall were washed away. In the 1960s a mini wall was constructed near the tramway. Further works along the coast have seen the town protected by a continuous line of walling. These mass concrete defences are 14 feet thick at the base and 5 feet thick at the neckings.

Right: Pictured in 1980, the ABC on Church Street was one of only two cinemas still open in the town as the end of the last century approached, the other being the Odeon. In the heyday of the silver screen during the 1930s, some 18 movie houses could be found in Blackpool and Fleetwood. They were popular places to do your courting. A bespectacled lad we know took his latest lass onto the back row. He whispered to her, 'Are we watching the film or what?' With a bit of luck, she did not hear him and replied, 'What?' His glasses were soon in his pocket. However, usherettes were always on hand to shine their torches along the seats, so ensuring that hanky did not materialise into panky. 'Going to the flicks', as many of us knew it, was quite good value for money. There were nearly always two films to be watched, along with a newsreel, a short documentary and a cartoon. The Empire Theatre was built in 1895 and was renamed the Hippodrome in 1929, which coincided with the arrival of talkies in the cinema. Silent films were first shown there in 1910, but the Empire/Hippodrome continued to double as a theatre and cinema for several decades before closing in 1960. It was largely rebuilt and relaunched as the ABC Theatre

on 31 May, 1963, when Cliff Richard and the Shadows topped the bill. Televised shows, such as Blackpool Night Out, were transmitted from here. Stars such as Frank Ifield, Morecambe and Wise, Cilla Black and Engelbert Humperdinck were brought into our living rooms in the 1960s as they performed on the ABC stage. The theatre was converted into a triple screen cinema in 1981, before the owners called it a day in 1998. It is now the Syndicate Night Club.

Above: Looking along the pedestrianised street towards the promenade, the 'wonder of Woolies' on the right is something we thought would be with us forever. The original five and ten cent store that sold all manner of cheap and cheerful goods had developed into a global chain. Frank Winfield Woolworth opened his first store in Utica, New York, in 1878. The company came to Britain in the early 20th century when a store was opened in Liverpool. Soon, there was a Woolworth's in just about every town in the land. To see the company crash, its outlets close and the shelves emptied in 2008 and early 2009 was as if a little bit of ourselves and our childhood had been axed. No more pick 'n' mix and no more questions from girls on the counters asking, 'How much is it, love?'

ALONG THE
PROM

Although Blackpool has a reputation for being a lively and bustling sort of place, there are plenty of oases of calm and relaxation that can be found without too much effort. This was appreciated by those who helped plan and design various features along the front, including this part of South Shore. In the 1890s it was estimated that Blackpool's 7,000 dwellings could accommodate 250,000 holidaymakers, as well as the permanent population of 35,000. These visitors required entertaining, and the period saw the development of many of the resort's famous attractions. However, consideration was given to those who perceived that entertainment could be given in quieter surroundings that were more pleasing on the eye than kiss me quick hats and toffee apples. Various garden areas were created, such as the Rockery Promenade we see here. The greenery, developed in the 1920s, provided a soothing antidote to the garish colours elsewhere. Each of the gardens had its own character. Some included putting greens and tennis courts, but the rock garden in the photograph was a particularly pleasant spot. It even had its own stream of water that trickled out from a weeping cave. You could not help but feel rested and relaxed in this environment. Bliss.

Above: There is a modern Gynn Hotel on Dickson Street, not far from where this photograph was taken. But, the old Gynn Inn actually stood on what is now referred to as Gynn Square, on the corner of Gynn Street, until it was demolished on 2 May 1921. The whitewashed pub was one of the most recognisable landmarks and popular watering hole for earlier generations.

Originally a 16th century farmhouse, it had dispensed ale and bonhomie for well over a century before being regarded as surplus to needs. This view looking away along Queen's Promenade and towards Bispham comes from the period just after the inn disappeared. The open topped motorcars belonged to wealthy members of the middle classes or better as these were

definitely luxury items in the roaring 20s. Land on the former Gynn estate was purchased in the late 19th century by a group of local businessmen. Most of the hotels and housing along the front of this northern part of the town dates from around the turn of the century. The road rises as you head away. There used to be more substantial cliffs in the distance, but they were reduced as the stone within them was used to help fill in the new northern promenade. A large roundabout is now in place at this spot in the foreground.

Above: At least there was one spot where it was made clear that dogs were not welcome. The notice in the paddling pool made it abundantly clear to Fido's owners that their beloved pooch was not wanted here. Without the assistance of man's best friend youngsters loved to splash around happily in this environment. Their parents took the weight off their feet for a while as they settled down for a spot of rest and relaxation before it was time to dry the kids off and head back to the guest house. This general view was taken around 1930, just after the wave of developments along South Shore had been undertaken. The new South Promenade and Stanley Park were both unveiled in 1926 by the Earl of Derby. The former project was part of a four year plan that saw the promenade extended from Victoria Pier right up to the boundary with St Annes. A series of decorative, sunken gardens was formed along the 25 foot wide footpath that ran alongside the sea wall that protected promenaders from the spray of the breakers rolling in from the Irish Sea.

Left: The old brick built Customs' Watch House at the mouth of the River Wyre estuary had been turned into a sea front shop after its usefulness in official circles was over. Potential customers scurried by on this blustery and slightly chilly day during the summer of 1935. It was not the best of weather for enjoying an ice cream. When looking at a scene from so long ago it is heart warming to know that some things have not changed. Take a stroll along this part of the promenade at Fleetwood today and the very same little shop is still standing, continuing to dispense ice cream to visitors whose great-grandparents may well be in this photograph. Just beyond the Watch House, the ferry terminal can be seen. This still operates a service to Larne in County Antrim and, occasionally, Douglas on the Isle of Man. There are also crossings to Knott End-on-Sea, the village that is just a short hop across the river.

Above: The lights twinkled like little stars as they illuminated the early evening panorama. Dusk promenaders enjoyed the moment. The daytime crowds had left or were taking tea in their guest house and the night-time revellers had yet to make an appearance. It was a peaceful time in which to reflect upon on a day well spent and an opportunity to look forward to the rest of the evening. Plans could be discussed and decisions made. The Tower could be seen from most vantage points along the front, rising some 518 feet above the ground. Its impressive frame contains 3,478 tons of steel and 352 tons of cast iron, with a 60 foot flagpole adorning its peak. Workmen use nine tons of paint whenever its exterior needs decorating. During the autumn, when the Illuminations are in full swing, as many as 10,000 light bulbs are used to adorn the structure.

Bottom right: Even if the weather was not at its best, there was no way that holidaymakers or day trippers on the front were going to do anything else other than enjoy the day at the seaside.

Carefully wrapped up against a stiff breeze, they took advantage of the seating to catch up on the latest news from home or abroad. When their limbs got just a little stiff, then a stroll along one of the piers would soon get the circulation going. North Pier, the first and longest of Blackpool's trio, opened on 21 May 1863. At its most accommodating time, there was room for over 3,000 to sit along the length of its 2,130 feet. In typical Victorian speak, it was planned to 'afford greater promenading space of the most invigorating kind'.

Top right: The Girl Pat who was the subject of the penny a peep show through the telescope was not some form of 1930s' striptease artist. It was actually the name of a fishing boat that had a brief period of notoriety. The boat was a 70ft seiner, a small fishing boat skippered by 'Dod' Osborne. He and his six man crew fished out of Grimsby, but formed the belief that, because of poor returns,

the owners were about to decommission the vessel and throw the captain and crew out of work. Osborne came up with a hare brained solution. He decided to take the 'Girl Pat' and his men out across the Atlantic to South America where they could find work ferrying cargo. Osborne sailed his boat to West Africa where he refuelled and took on provisions, charging everything to the owners back on Humberside. The next port of call should have been the Azores, but the captain's navigational skills were not up to cross-ocean sailing and the 'Girl Pat' missed its stop. By now, the game was up and a hue and cry had been launched. Somehow the tired and hungry sailors managed to make it to Georgetown in what was then British Guiana. They were down on food, fuel and their luck as arrest was immediate. On 19 October 1937, they were found guilty of larceny. Osborne was sentenced to 18 months' hard labour. The public was intrigued and regarded the affair as something of a Robin Hood style adventure. The boat was brought back to Blighty and put on show at Blackpool and other popular seaside resorts. Visitors were charged for being allowed

to look round the boat. You might say that in the two years before the war began, she made far more money for her owners than when she was fishing in the North Sea. Osborne served in the Royal Navy with credit during the war, but later fell on hard times and committed suicide in Paris in the 1950s.

Above: As war became inevitable, civil defence measures started to be taken to help defend our country from aerial attack and possible invasion. Newsreels showing footage from the Spanish Civil War had alerted us to the perils we faced when the Luftwaffe came to call. Gas masks were issued and training given on how to react when, rather than if, an air raid happened. Some houses had their own Anderson shelters built in their back gardens, while in towns and cities places were designated as underground shelters or purpose built ones were erected. This one was put in place at the start of the war, opposite the Golden Mile. The young mother, looking like a prototype Andrews' sister, cast a puzzled glance at the contraption. Thankfully, she would never need to use it as Blackpool was spared. This was surprising as, in addition to the obvious industrial targets, Hitler deliberately ordered attacks on places of interest to the general public in an effort to lower morale. Places such as York and Coventry were among those selected in what became known as the Baedeker Raids. It now appears that our town was omitted because the German leader had plans to turn it into a centre where his all conquering troops could relax and enjoy themselves. He had visions of paratroopers landing in Stanley Park and marching in triumph along the promenade. However, we did not know that at the time and so precautions were taken and defences were built. Concrete blocks were placed in strategic positions to thwart

invaders and posts protruded from the sands to deter pilots from attempting to land on the beach.

Bottom left: By 1958, Britain was starting to get back on its feet after the prolonged period of austerity after the war. Even Prime Minister Macmillan was moved to say that 'We have never had it so good'. This may have been something of an exaggeration, but we certainly were better off than we had been in the depressing days of the 1930s. Blackpool was bursting with visitors that summer, even if every day was not blessed with sunshine. From the coats and caps on display, it would seem that this particular day was one on which to keep moving. Still, there were always the amusement arcades to pop into if it rained. There were those machines where you might get lucky and win a three week old Mars bar, if your ball bearing went into the right slot. Alternatively, there were the 'penny falls' where we added our coppers to a growing pile that just would not tip over the edge for us. The one with the mechanical grabbing arm was always the most frustrating, you were determined to win something, but never quite got it spot on. The

Lounge Bar at the Wellington on Chapel Street, opposite Central Pier, attracted some drinkers, but most were happy just to sit around and chat. A MacDonald's and the Jewel on the Mile stand on this corner today, just across from Happy Dayz.

Below: Once over, spending a penny meant precisely that. What is now a euphemism for going to the toilet initially described the cost of what we shall tastefully call the procedure. Most towns built their central public toilets in, what can accurately be called, the bowels of the earth. Men disappeared down the Gents at one end of the designated section, while ladies went down the steps at the opposite end. Of course, the latter bitterly complained that their visit always cost them money while men, more often than not, escaped scot free. The toilets on Central Promenade were photographed in 1958. The telephone box by the Ladies is also a period piece. The telephone system inside the box had a large container on top of which the handset rested. A caller inserted his fourpence into a slot and dialled the required number. On hearing someone on the other end of the line, a shiny, silvery button marked 'A' on the black container was depressed. The coppers fell into the heart of the contraption and a connection to the recipient of the call was completed. If there was no reply, the caller pressed a button marked 'B' and his money was returned. Future entrepreneurs, bankers and wide boys always pressed Button B on entering the phone box as it was remarkable how often that the previous user had forgotten to collect his cash after an unanswered call.

Right: The Lifeboat Station on Central Promenade, seen in 1958, is presently one of only two stations in the country to be equipped with three inshore lifeboats. It was established in 1864. Coxswain Robert Bickerstaffe was one of the first in a long line of Blackpool lifeboatmen to receive an award for gallantry. In 1880, he won the silver medal for his part in saving four lives on the doomed Fleetwood schooner, the 'Bessie Jones'. Noted as one of the most memorable and difficult rescues for the crew of the Blackpool lifeboat 'Robert William'. The wreck of the Bessie Jones prompted a campaign which resulted in St Annes obtaining a lifeboat. The station seen here was opened in 1937 by the Duke of Kent who gave his name to one of the lifeboats. A futuristic looking new one was completed in 1998 and it combines the station with a visitors' centre.

comes in the shape of the crowns that can be seen all along this stretch of the Golden Mile. This is jubilee year when we celebrated 25 years of Queen Elizabeth's reign on the British throne. Although the actual date of her silver anniversary was 6 February, we could hardly have expected her to rejoice on the anniversary of her father's death. Consequently, the nation waited until June when the monarch set the ball rolling for a week of festivities by lighting a giant bonfire in Windsor Park. Prophets of doom and gloom warned that the country would largely ignore the occasion as they were fed up with funding the monarchy. Not a bit of it. Out came the trestle tables, portable record players and home made savouries as street parties were held that were reminiscent of VE Day.

Above left: It was Fay Wray who played the part of the heroine, Ann Darrow, in the 1933 film 'King Kong'. The scene where the gorilla holds her in one hand, as he sits astride the mast on top of the Empire State Building while planes buzz about him, is one of cinema's magical moments. To see his reincarnation part way up Blackpool Tower in 1984 was something of a surprise to those not in the know as they strolled the pavement beneath. The one ton structure was made from 22,750 square feet of vinyl coated nylon and stood 84 feet in height. Borrowed from its home in San Diego as part of the Tower's 90th birthday celebrations. It was winched into place by workmen who had never seen the like before. The sight of the huge creature glaring down on passers-by should have been enough to make young children have nightmares, but they seemed to take it all in their stride. King Kong did not outstay his welcome. He was in place for 17 days before being shipped back to California. Fay Wray died in 2004, the year before a remake of her most famous movie was released.

Left: The tram's destination, Starr Gate, is the southern terminus of the line, close to Squires Gate Station and the airport. There, the trams change direction without changing ends by means of a single track loop. It gets its name from the spiky or 'starr' grass that grows there and helps bond the sand dunes together. The scene is obviously from the summer of 1977. The couple in the foreground, with their flared trousers, help us date what we can see. However, the biggest pointer

BLACKPOOL F.C.

Blackpool F.C. was one of the leading lights in English soccer for two decades after the last war, competing for major trophies and providing the home countries with international players. For a while, it could rival the big guns from the large cities and a visit from the seasiders often provided the host club with a busy set of turnstiles that particular Saturday afternoon. The club was founded in 1887 when a breakaway group left St John's FC and later joined the Lancashire League where it met with some success, leading to the title in its fourth season of membership. Blackpool's home matches were played at Raikes Hall Gardens and attracted crowds of around 2,000. This provided a financial base that encouraged a successful application to join the Football League in 1896. The club moved to Stanley Park for about a year before finding its next home at Gamble's Field, Bloomfield Road where it has been ever since.

The photograph of Bloomfield Road was taken on 10 September, 1938, at the start of what was to turn out to be the last full season of proper professional soccer for seven years. Twelve months on and war would have been declared, German tanks have rolled across Europe and thousands of British children rushed out of the cities and into the countryside as evacuees. Prime Minister Chamberlain was contemplating flying out to Munich for appeasement talks with Herr Hitler on the day that 29,128 spectators, with the packed Spion Kop, crammed into Bloomfield Road to watch the game against Aston Villa. This was a fairly large crowd for this ground, but not unusually so for the times as a regular attendance of over 25,000 was the norm. The biggest turnout took place on 17 September 1955 when 38,098 came along for the visit of Stan Cullis's powerful Wolverhampton Wanderers. Of course, nowadays the health and safety restrictions and remodelling of the old terraces and provision of seating means that the current capacity is just under 10,000. The 'Oh be joyful' motto on top of the main stand referred to OBJ, a brand of bottled ale brewed by Dutton's of Blackburn. It was a stronger beer, with a bottle costing a few coppers more than a pint of mild. Drinkers supped it sparingly because of the cost as well as the strength.

The Seasiders were relegated after three seasons in the top flight, but bounced back in 1937 under manager Joe Smith. He was to oversee some of Blackpool's most productive times in the 23 years he spent in the hot seat. Although doing well in the league, it was the FA Cup that was to provide the most magical moments after the war.

The picture top right was taken on 24 April, 1948. 100,000 spectators walked down Olympic Road as Wembley Way was known in honour of the Games coming to London that year. However, they were not interested in events later that summer. It was not Emil Zatopek or Fanny Blankers-Koen who were the star attractions on that day, but two sides from the northwest of England. Blackpool faced Manchester United in what was to be a classic of free flowing football that would not be bettered for many a year. There was no crowd trouble, just a stream of football fans enjoying the day out, exchanging friendly banter with people of like mind who supported their team but were able to applaud an opponent's success, albeit grudgingly.

It was just laps of the ground, running up and down the terracing and cutting back on the fags that got the boys on the right in shape. From the left are Eddie Shimwell, Stan Mortensen

The famous tangerine strip was worn with little distinction over the next 30 years as the successive sides that turned out could only manage a modest series of results as the club languished in the second division. With manager Harry Evans at the helm and the free scoring Jimmy Hampson banging in goals for fun, Blackpool won its first major honour in 1929-30 when it lifted the Division Two title. Hampson was a formidable goalscorer. In the late 1920s he netted 101 times in just 97 games. Such striking prowess would earn him millions of pounds a year in today's inflated wage structure. Tragically, he drowned in a fishing accident in 1938, aged just 31. His total of 252 goals in 373 games for the club is still a record.

George Dick, Jimmy McIntosh, Joe Robinson, Ronnie Suart, Hughie Kelly, Stan Matthews, Harry Johnston, Walter Rickett, Eric Hayward and Alec Munro. Suart and McIntosh did not make the team for Wembley. They watched from the stand as Shimwell opened the scoring and for Mortensen to restore the lead by half time after Rowley equalised for United. However, three opposition goals in the last 20 minutes saw Blackpool lose a thrilling encounter by 4-2.

The Blackpool team that took to the field that day was: Robinson, Shimmwell, Crosland, Johnston, Haywood, Kelly, Matthews, Munroe, Mortensen, Dick, and Rickett. They returned to Wembley in 1951, but were unlucky to run into a top class Newcastle United team. With Jackie Milburn in his prime, it was no wonder that the Magpies were victorious 2-0, with Wor Jackie notching both goals. A diminutive inside right, Ernie Taylor, starred in the Geordie side. He was transferred to Blackpool six months later and went on to play in the 1953

final as well as another one in 1958 in Manchester United's Munich ravaged side.

That year of the Coronation saw more television sets purchased than ever before. Those who got them in good time for the ceremony in June were able to witness one of the most romantic of Cup Finals, though Bolton Wanderers' fans have never subscribed to that notion.

Pictured right is the the squad that reached the FA Cup Final yet again on 2 May 1953. Back row: E Shimwell, H Johnston, G Farm, J Crosland, C Robinson, A Brown. Centre row: J Smith (manager), S Matthews, E Taylor, S Mortensen, J Mudie, W Perry, J Lynas (trainer). Front row: E Fenton, G McKnight, H Kelly, T Garrett.

The unlucky ones who missed out on an appearance were Brown, McKnight, Crosland and Kelly. There had been the equivalent of today's hype about the match as the highly regarded Stan Matthews was playing at the ripe old age of 38 and this would probably be his last chance of a winner's medal. We all know now that he went on to play for England when he was 40 and for Stoke City as a 50 year old, but at the time this was seen to be his swansong.

The game started poorly for Blackpool as Nat Lofthouse scored after just 90 seconds. Mortensen equalised, but goals either side of halftime saw Bolton take a 3-1 lead. However, the Trotters were handicapped as Bell was injured and little more than a passenger. There were no substitutes in those days and Blackpool started to take territorial control. Mortensen completed his hat trick and, with extra time looming, Matthews escaped yet again down the right. Deep into injury time, his cross (pictured below) cut out the Bolton right half, Johnny Wheeler, and left winger Bill Perry was on hand to slide in the winner at the far post. A remarkable turn around gave us a 4-3 victory.

The team made the traditional open topped bus tour (top right) of its home town on board one of the Seagull Coaches that regularly provided the transport to away games. Skipper Harry Johnston proudly held the Cup aloft as a tour of the Fylde coast culminated in a reception at the Town Hall in front of 15,000 fans. Sadly, that was to be the last time a major piece of silverware was won by Blackpool FC, though the days in the big time were not over just yet.

club's highest ever league position when they finished as First Division (then the top flight in England) runners-up in the 1955-56 season. Playing behind the great Stanley Matthews gave him the opportunity to become one of the first overlapping full-backs. His undoubted skill was noticed and in 1959 Armfield was voted Young Player of the Year. In 1966, he narrowly lost out to Bobby Charlton for the Footballer of the Year award and had to content himself with being Blackpool's Player of the Year. He endured little success in his seventeen years with the Seasiders, the club having won the

In 1956 we ended the season as runners-up to the mighty Busby Babes and carried on giving other Division One teams a run for their money into the 1960s, helped by such burgeoning talent as Alan Ball, a future England star. The run at the top could not last and relegation came along at last in 1967. The team returned to the first division in 1970 for a single season before dropping out once more. By 1978 we were in Division Three and three years later the ignominy of life in Division Four was experienced. Blackpool escaped from the basement in the mid 1980s and has spent the last quarter of a century in the equivalent of Leagues Two and Three. The good old days when we had four players in the same England team, as we did in 1953 when Matthews, Mortensen, Johnston and Taylor played, have long gone. Indeed, it is over 40 years since the likes of Ball, Armfield and Waiters won England caps, but we can still dream.

Player profile: James Christopher 'Jimmy' Armfield (right) earned the respect of his peers during a distinguished Football League career at Blackpool. After Armfield's family moved to Blackpool from Denton, he was spotted in a practice match at Bloomfield Road by then-Tangerines manager Joe Smith. Impressed, Smith offered him a trial. On 27 December 1954, Armfield made his Blackpool debut at Portsmouth. He was part of the Blackpool side that finished in what is to date still the

FA Cup the year prior to his arrival. The exception was promotion to the First Division in 1969-70. He would remain a one-club man throughout his playing career. Others, notably goalkeeper Gordon West, Alan Ball and Emlyn Hughes would be sold, however, in order to balance the books, and the clubs fortunes inevitably suffered. Armfield was awarded a testimonial match, played on 2 September, 1970, his 35th birthday, and thousands turned out to pay tribute to him. He played his final game for Blackpool on 1 May, 1971, in front of a crowd of over 30,000 against Manchester United at Bloomfield Road. During his playing days, Armfield was

called 'Gentlemen Jim', probably because he was never sent off in 626 games for Blackpool, 43 appearances for England and nine Under-23 internationals. Incredibly, he was booked just once, for two successive fouls in an FA Cup tie against Norwich. Although born in Denton, Armfield has spent most of his life living in Blackpool, moving there in a World War II evacuation, and in 2003 he was awarded the freedom of the resort. Among many other accolades he has received, on 18 September, 2008, Armfield was awarded a place in the football Hall of Fame at the National Football Museum in Preston, joining fellow former Seasiders Stanley Matthews and Stan Mortensen in the list of Blackpool players selected.

ON THE BEACH

Left: No day at the seaside would be complete without an ice cream. Splash on some raspberry and let the juice and the melting confectionery run down your fingers, Perfect. 'Stop me and buy one' was a familiar slogan in the interwar years. Originally used by Walls' salesmen riding tricycles fitted with refrigerated units, the motto was often purloined by other members of the same trade peddling differently branded ices. Warrick box trikes, used to carry ice cream, were first seen on the streets of London in 1923. Cecil Rodd, a Walls' employee, came up with the advertising slogan that was to be part of the English language for the next half century. This method of selling ice cream, that superseded the now traditional van, was initially so successful that Walls' sales of £13,000 in 1924 increased to £440,000 in just three years. When war came in 1939, ice cream manufacture was severely restricted because of the limitations imposed by rationing. The tricycles were, somewhat strangely, requisitioned by the military. Perhaps it was intended that the Home Guard use them to practise anti tank warfare. In 1947, Walls sold off its tricycle fleet of over 3,000 machines and invested in new freezers for shops. The pedalling ice cream salesmen was still seen on occasion in the 1950s, but became something of a rarity by the end of that decade.

Above: It did not matter what you wore or what the weather did. If you came to the seaside, then you had to sit on the sands. Deckchairs and rugs covered almost every square inch of the golden stuff and, even if the gales blew and the rain threatened to fall, men pulled down the caps that bit tighter over their foreheads and the womenfolk wrapped their coats a little bit tighter around them. This was holiday week and they were determined to have it on the beach, come hail or shine. Wish you

Above: It is possible that Paddy and his oyster cart had a relative in Dublin selling cockles and mussels, alive alive-oh. It is hard to imagine what the bobby in full uniform was doing patrolling the beach, unless some wag had told him that the breakers from the Irish Sea were up to no good and could be classed as crime waves! Whatever his purpose, the trio next to him steadfastly ignored his presence. The young man obviously thought that he was whatever the 1950 word was for 'cool' in his quite remarkable 'shades'. The girls must have been from a milltown. Where else would they have learned to tie those turbans that, during the working day, protected their hair from the machinery and the flying shuttles? This was probably one of the Wakes' Weeks common in Lancashire towns. They originated as religious holidays commemorating holy days and festivals, but were adopted during the Industrial Revolution by communities nominating certain weeks as their holiday breaks. Wakes' Weeks also became the focus for fairs, but with the advent of the railway, whole towns shut down during this special period. Large swathes of the neighbourhood were emptied as the population packed into railway carriages and headed off to the seaside for the annual bash. The workers were hell bent on packing as much enjoyment as they could into such a short time. After all, the memories had to last for another 12 months.

Right: It was expected that every trip to the seaside included an ice cream and a ride on a donkey. The former is still around in plentiful supply, but the opportunity to get on Neddy's back is one that comes along less often than it used to. These comical looking animals have always been popular with children as their sedate and steady gait has meant that a ride on their backs offers little in the way of harm, but a lot in the way of enjoyment. It is thought

that the first time that donkeys took to the beach was in about 1890 at Margate. Some of the regulations surrounding their deployment on Blackpool beach sound rather amusing. One set goes under the pompous title of 'Regulations with reference to asses on the foreshore'. This is known colloquially as the 'Donkey Charter', but it does have some sensible rules and recommendations. No person over 16 years of age or weighing in excess of 8 stone is permitted to have a ride. Friday was designated as the Donkey Sabbath, namely a day of rest.

Left: I've come to the seaside and I am bloomin' well going to enjoy it. I cannot possibly go back home without having had a dip, so here goes. Well, that is the shins nice and salty and now is the time to dry them off, get the sand out of my toes and my boots and socks back on. I do love a holiday at the seaside. There is nothing quite like it. Quick, get the suncream on those calves. The last time these legs saw the sun was when King George was a lad.

Does my bum look big in this? This lass has all the potential for giving lads a tough time. Not only is she very pretty, but she also knows it. Look out, boys. She was obviously well aware of modern fashion. Her modern, knitted two piece was designed more to catch the eye than for practical purposes. The fabric would have got rather heavy and sag somewhat when immersed in the sea. Anyway, she was more interested in making waves among the males on the sands. The first modern two piece was created by Louis Réard in 1946, naming it the bikini after the atoll where atomic bomb tests were carried out. Réard reasoned that the costume's effects would be akin to that of a nuclear reaction and he was not far wrong. It blew some men's brains apart. However, more modest two piece costumes, like the one seen here, had been modelled in the early 1940s by such movie stars as Ava Gardner, Lana Turner and Rita Hayworth. This lovely on the golden sands at Blackpool could dream that she was in the same league as those doyennes of the silver screen. Maybe it was not just reverie because she obviously had the all the basic ingredients and they were all in the right places as well.

Below: The pram on the beach alongside the ice cream cart looks to be quite a stylish one, possibly a Silver Cross. It would have set mum back more than a few bob or it might have been a gift from a proud grandparent. Silver Cross first began designing transport for babies back in 1877. It all began when former postman William Wilson combined his ideas for an innovative spring suspension system with a handy reversible hood, and invented the modern pram. Little is known about William Wilson but what we do know is that he was a prolific inventor and engineer, who started his own business making postal carts and perambulators at Silver Cross Street, Hunslet, Leeds. In the 20's Silver Cross was crowned the No1 manufacturer of baby carriages for Royals when the Wilson brothers supplied a Silver Cross baby carriage to George VI and Queen Elizabeth, The Queen Mother. In 1951 they launched a series of new iconic shaped prams, promoted through a series of posters, often portraying a Silver Cross pram alongside a Rolls Royce car.

Below: They had survived the Great War and got through the privations of the 1939-45 hostilities. This couple represented a generation born and raised under Queen Victoria who had seen so much change. The carnage of two world wars must have affected them, but on top of that there were the major changes in their

everyday lives that they had experienced and to which they had to adapt. They saw the first motor cars and aeroplanes. They listened to the first records on turntables and marvelled at talking pictures on movie screens. Antibiotics and medicines had helped prolong their lives and the newly instituted National Health Service was going to assist them further. Is it any wonder that they were feeling just a little bit whacked and needed a few minutes lost in themselves? Let us hope that the photographer of this late 1940s' scene tiptoed quietly away after recording a well earned moment of peace and happiness. John Darby and his wife, Joan, were first mentioned in a Henry Woodfall poem in 1735 and revived by Lord Byron who commented on them in 1812. However, it was the Victorian poet Francis Weatherby who cemented Darby and Joan in our vocabulary when he wrote of them, 'Hand in hand when our life was May. Hand in hand when our hair is grey'.

This lady is struggling to get baby settled, but it was a difficult journey across the sand. The pram wheels were made for pavements, not beaches, and the contraption was heavy enough in its own right. The collapsible, aluminium pushchair was not invented until the mid 1960.

Below: At first glance it would seem that this youngster was doing something rather unmentionable. Fortunately, we have it on good authority that the child was taking a photograph of mum and grandparents. The promenade in the distance provided a good backdrop to this holiday scene from around 1950. Nowadays, we can take countless photographs with our digital cameras. We point and click repeatedly. At that rate, we are guaranteed the one good image that we need out of the hundred we have taken. The other 99 can be discarded at just a touch of the delete button. One of the joys of being on holiday has been lost. We no longer have those few days of limbo after returning from our two weeks away when we were on tenterhooks having handed over a roll of film to the chemist. Removing the roll from the back of the camera was a carefully carried out exercise as we did not want to get any light into the film. We put the record of our holiday into a little can and went off down the High Street and gave the pharmacist the privilege

of transferring our negatives onto photographic paper. Later in the week we returned and anxiously opened up the packet of prints. A successful outcome was not guaranteed because some would be overexposed and others disappointing as we had pointed the camera towards the sun. Occasionally, there would be a close up of the photographer's thumb, but there were just enough satisfactory ones to make us grin from ear to ear as they had captured the moment beautifully. Now we could bore our friends and neighbours with them. Well, we had had to yawn through theirs. At least no-one in our immediate circle owned a ciné camera.

Above: Once you had claimed your square yard of sand, that was it for the day, come hell, high water or the occasional rainstorm. Deckchairs were erected, albeit with some difficulty as the contraptions always seemed to have a knack of taking a chunk out of your fingers. The kids scrabbled around in the sand with their buckets and spades and mum smiled benignly and offered little bits of advice or warnings about making sure they knew where the family was if they wandered off. The menfolk gazed out to sea passively, just happy that they had a week away from the shop floor. If the sun shone, those with flat caps were fine. They pulled them out of their pockets and plonked them squarely on their heads. It was the hatless ones who provided their own peculiar fashion statements. Whatever the temperature, the jacket stayed firmly in place, but the head was protected in a variety of ways. Some opted for the hankie, with a knot tied at each corner. Then there was the tea towel. Quite how this managed to get itself packed is a mystery, but it found its way onto the beach year after year. The newspaper made a good titfer. Either opened at the middle page and placed aloft or carefully crafted into a Robin Hood style by the use of Lancastrian origami, it did its job.

NOW THEN!
...the way we were

Each generation thinks of itself as 'modern', at every stage of life and yet we are all relics and momentoes of our own history. As time goes by, we try to hang on to our more modish and fashionable behaviour and attitudes, sometimes with the thought that we can defy the passing of time, despite our constant creation of 'the past' and our own archaeology. Most people, however, enjoy looking back and remembering with affection things done, things achieved and comparing the context of their early lives with 'improvements' made (sometimes!) in more recent times. Things often seem not to be as good as in the 'olden days', but most of the time we are not looking at a level playing field. Inevitably, many of our childhood memories, whatever our age now, are of endless summers and snow-filled

winters, a sort of 'local to us' and historically appropriate version of Dylan Thomas's 'A Child's Christmas in Wales'! But for all of us, time marches on and as we get older, it seems strange that we find ourselves attempting to explain to an eleven year old god-daughter that there WAS life, of a sort, before computers, emphasising simultaneously our incredibly ancient origins! Wartime experiences and memories often define generations although with involvement in more recent conflicts, even this time line has had to be redefined. The progress in radio and TV development has outstripped most people's imagination and provided a sometimes obsessive and questionable way of 'stuffing' our days. Until the middle of the twentieth century, children often had to use their own imagination, inventiveness and

All the equipment and artefacts used in play were simple, often loud and often extremely irritating in their use and application, but GREAT fun!

Left: In the 1950's, toys were still quite simple, for boys and girls. In a society that still placed the emphasis on women as home makers and 'children producers', toymakers were still making a lot of money from selling pretty little dolls to pretty little girls, banking on their softness for small, defenceless creatures in their own image. This wonderful picture, taken in 1950, shows two such little girls enjoying posing for a 'family' photograph, repeated no doubt, twenty years later, as the 'real thing'! Note the grittily determined, no-nonsense expression of the young lady at the back and the rather shyer, slightly myopic expression of the seated young lady with hair that, possibly, she has spent the rest of her life not being able to 'do a thing with'.!

Below: The influence of Errol Flynn in the 1940's is obvious here in a game involving bows and arrows. His playing of Robin Hood against Olivia de Havilland as Maid Marian, had a ground-breaking impact, for some little boys, that remained with them to their teenage years (and in some cases even longer!). Cinema has always had an influence on children's re-enactment and performance of stories and fables. Certainly children in the 1940's rarely complained about boredom or having 'nothing to do'. They simply grasped the nettle and worked out what they could turn it into and they did it together!

creativity. The streets were filled with groups of children of different ages pretending to be somebody, somewhere and something else. This was fun for most, freeing and gentle in its stimulation and engendered a relevant and satisfactory competitiveness conducive to learning.

Facing page: Outside, including in the playground, improvisation was the name of the game. You didn't need a ball for football - a tightly bound bundle of rags or clothes would do. There were games that matched the seasons, conkers for example. Those determined to win used foul and dishonest ways to convert the simple conker into a hard and unyielding boulder to cheat their way to success! Later in the year it was marbles with wonderful 'glass beads' put to aggressive and destructive use to determine 'top dog'. There were also 'collecting' activities, usually involving cards with familiar faces, often footballers or film stars. Playground games were often determined by gender, with the differences usually marked by the polarising of physical prowess and single-mindedness on the one hand and a softer camaraderie and togetherness on the other.

Above: These young ladies were la crème de la crème, as Miss Jean Brodie might have put it. Blackpool Girls' High School offered young women the opportunity to make their mark on the world. Many thought that horizons for girls should be set at office and secretarial work, or perhaps nursing or teaching. Fortunately, there were others who had loftier ambitions for their charges and directed them towards universities and colleges of further and higher education where top professional courses could be followed. Before that, there was the daily grind in the classroom. There was none of this modern trend of sitting around a table, chatting with pals while you did whatever work you fancied. There were Latin primers to be studied, logarithm tables to be consulted and essays to be written in carefully formed Marion Richardson handwriting, using a proper fountain pen. At the end of it all were the examinations. There was no such thing as course work to be measured. Everything depended upon the examination papers that had to be answered. Teachers were strict and doled out punishments that were meant to keep girls on the straight and narrow. Boys were taboo and a wasteful distraction for any young lady of ambition. The pupils diligently worked at their tasks without question. Although it is an exaggeration to refer to these days as the happiest of their lives, they were certainly among the most formative.

Right: At one time, Monday was the traditional washday for many. For working class families, the burden fell upon 'mum'. Her role as a housewife meant that the day was spent boiling clothes in a tub and wringing them out through the mangle before pegging out on the line in the back yard. Before the days of sophisticated washing powders and rubber gloves, reddened hands were her reward and yet there were still beds to be made, carpets to beat and lino to wash. The children needed feeding and the evening meal had to be ready when 'dad' got home. It was hard work and there were few, if any, modern electrical appliances or 'white goods' to make the task of running the house any easier. Many families lived in terraced housing, some of it back to back, with outdoor 'lavvies', where you learned to whistle with one foot against the door in case someone else attempted to enter this little smelly enclave of privacy. Many houses still had a tin bath that was dragged in from the yard and filled with kettle after kettle of boiling water before family members took it in turn to soak themselves. This photograph, dating from the 1950's, shows a typical scene from life at the time; families and communities were close knit, sharing each other's joys and sorrows. It was quite common to lend a neighbour a helping hand in times of need and this was often more than just a cup of sugar. Friendships were often formed that lasted a lifetime.

Right: Conditions may have been grim on occasions, but in any Lancashire street there was usually time for a warm smile and friendly chat. These were the days when people routinely left their doors unlocked - or open, without fear of someone running off with their television. Of course, they didn't have a television, but you know what we mean! These days the neighbourly culture which we used to take for granted has disappeared from many areas and some people seem to know the characters in the popular soap operas better than the people next door. It would be unusual, to say the least, to see a modern housewife scrubbing the pavement outside her house.

Right: Fashion on the beach has surely changed a lot over the last one hundred years. Appropriate beach wear for men and women has moved with fashion. At one time, wool was, amazingly, seen as a suitable fabric for bathing outfits, despite its hideous stretching and shapeless qualities. Topless men on the beach were seen, at one time, as rather racy and promiscuous; yet, how would our Victorian forebears have dealt with the increased promiscuity of the last twenty years, with men AND women prepared to do and bare anything and everything on a beach; they would have been horrified never mind amused! In those days, young women were very bold if they revealed their ankles, knees and arms as they changed, on their parent's insistence, into their bathing attire inside a bathing

cart that could be wheeled into the water. Discretion was everything and a lack of it irreversible and so morality and prudence were established and preserved! A hundred years from now, however, we can be certain that OUR successors will look back with equal, if not increased, incredulity at our take on what is appropriate or not to wear on a beach!

Below: Out of necessity, road safety has become a major issue for all of us in our lifetimes and has been written into the school curriculum since the middle of the twentieth century. As we can

see in photographs from the turn of the twentieth century which appear in this book, children played games in the streets and rode their bicycles on the carriageway with little danger to life or limb. With the steadily increasing traffic in the 1930's, safety became an obvious and challenging issue and with accident statistics rising alarmingly the government of the day was obliged to take action. Driving tests were introduced, Belisha Beacon crossings appeared in towns and cities and that well-known bestseller, The Highway Code was formulated and published. After the Second World War, local councils turned their attention to the protection of children, who, at the time, lacked awareness of the dangers that existed in merely crossing the road or cycling to the shops. In this photograph taken in 1950, youngsters are given instruction on a model roadway system. Stop, look and listen were watchwords drummed into children together with instruction on how to signal correctly and how to use crossings safely. Too many young people lost their lives through ignorance and generally the population were happy to see schemes, such as cycle proficiency, being promoted. In later years, we saw the Tufty Club, the Green Cross Code and, frighteningly, a fully permed Kevin Keegan advising us on why it was NOT a good idea to run out from behind parked cars! Sometimes, it all seemed a little light-hearted, but at least it aided the retention of this information in the heads of children.

Below: When Ernest Evans asked whether it was a bird or a plane up there and answered himself by telling us that it was a twister, a craze was born that swept dance floors across the western world. He also made sure that countless numbers of children would be embarrassed at weddings, 21st dos and parties during the 1990s as their parents risked hernias and heart attacks attempting to twist the night away whilst their offspring raised their eyes to heaven. Evans was a fan of the 1950s rocker Fats Domino and used his name as the inspiration for becoming known as Chubby Checker. Oddly, his first big hit in Britain was in 1963 with 'Let's Twist Again', a follow up to 'The Twist', a record that only became very popular the following year. By 1963, when this couple attempted to keep their seams straight as they girated in the front room to the music from their Dansette record player, Chubby's star had already begun to wane. He switched to the limbo in an effort to promote another dance form, but with limited success. Re-issues of his twist records have enjoyed new popularity in the intervening years, but have only added to the cringe factor for those forced to watch this couple 40 years on as they take the floor to the sound of 'Twist and Shout' or 'Peppermint Twist'. Sit down, mum, it's so gross.

ON THE MOVE

Cars, traps and trams sit easily alongside one another along the sea front. They have done so for more than a century and are likely to continue to do so for the foreseeable future. According to Marriott Edgar, half brother of the novelist Edgar Wallace, in his wonderful poem 'Albert and the Lion', Blackpool is 'noted for fresh air and fun'. Much of that can be experienced along the front. Taking a journey on an open top tram or being whisked along in a horse drawn carriage is a romantic and atmospheric way of seeing the Golden Mile and the sights that surround it. The town may be brash, but it is honest in its typically forthright manner that is northern to its roots. Blackpool seems to say that it knows visitors come in search of a good time and it is determined to satisfy that need. Traditional British pleasures by the bucket load?

Below: There may have been a war on, but this group of happy trippers was looking forward to some time at the seaside in August 1917. They had worked hard during the week and had more than done their bit for the war effort. Now they could take a little time out from the mundane things in life and block out the grim news from the trenches. Reality would soon dawn again, but in the meantime...

Right: The first decade of the last century was an exciting time for people who were determined to take to the air. For generations, man had striven to leave the ground and join the birds. All manner of fanciful contraptions had been tried from quaint machines, held together with little more than glue and a prayer, to weirdly feathered men frantically flapping their arms. Until the Wright brothers managed it, the resultant efforts of all their predecessors were summed up quite simply ...failure. Powered flight was restricted to balloons, kites and gliders. It was only after the successful trials at Kitty Hawk, North Carolina that the world truly believed that heavier than air machines could leave the ground and be powered and controlled

by mechanical means. After that fateful day in December 1903, aviators from all corners of the globe were copying the example of the American pioneers. The first flights only covered distances of a few yards, but the boundaries were soon being pushed back. Intrepid pilots took their lives in their own hands in the days before parachutes were invented. Louis Blériot (1872-1936) was one such daredevil and he flew the English Channel in 1909. By then, the public had become used to flocking to see air displays, like the one held that same year at this local pageant. Here, spectators were treated to a wonderful exhibition of flying in such marvellous machines as the Farman and Voisin biplanes. There were also Wright biplanes and early monoplanes, manufactured by Blériot or Antionette, for aviation fans to drool over. Blackpool was a popular centre for aerial thrills. Sir Alan Cobham's Flying Circus entertained thousands at a time during the 1920s and 1930s. It was he who once recommended Stanley Park as an airport site, rather than Squires Gate. Commercial flights were introduced on 24 May 1919 when AV Roe ran a daily service from the South Shore to Southport and Manchester.

Below: The line of single decker buses at the coach station was photographed not long before the outbreak of World War II. Back then, many of Blackpool's scheduled express coach services were served by Colosseum Coach Station. It was located on the seaward side of Blackpool Transport's bus garage, next to the tram depot, at South Shore. After its demolition, the site was used for Somerfield's supermarket. Lonsdale Road has now taken over the role of serving independent operators, while Blackpool Transport largely uses Corporation Street and Market Street as its interchange. The bus station at Talbot Road offers services to National Express and Stagecoach.

Above: Blackpool illuminations have been described as the 'greatest free show on earth'. They stretch for over 5 miles along the famous Blackpool Promenade and last for 65 nights from the beginning of September. The lights attract over 3.5 million visitors to the resort every year and as such are an essential part of British Heritage. A trip to see them has been one of the highlights of the year for thousands of people, who arrive by coach to tour through them. This Saturday morning scene was typical of many northern towns in the mid twentieth century, as the convoy of charra's set off splashing through the puddles to go to the famous resort. Possibly singing along to the Cascades 'Rhythm of the Rain' in 1962, the motorcade drove along Blackpool Road, passing Preston's Ashton Park. The three wheeler cars on the left of the picture are Bond mini's, manufactured on Ribbleton Lane in Preston and so beloved of Del Boys 'Only Fools and Horses'.

Right: The amount of candlepower used during the Illuminations' season does not bear thinking about, but how could we have Blackpool without them? A journey along the front in a handsome tram was just what the doctor ordered. The first tramcars ran on a track that was inaugurated on 29 September 1885. Initially powered by a conduit sited beneath road level, a form of plough was used to access the electric current via a central slot between the rails. This system was invented by Michael Holroyd-Smith (1848-1932), a Halifax man whose entrepreneurial potential was never fully appreciated. In the late 19th century he even expounded a theory for a helicopter, but was largely ignored. His method of electrifying trams was only briefly

successful in Blackpool. Sand blew into the groove in the trackway and this, allied with frequent short circuiting caused by the ingression of seawater, meant the temporary suspension of the service. In 1887, horse drawn trams were employed to replace the electrified ones. Perhaps this was an almost unique situation in the old replacing the new. Overhead cabling was introduced and Holroyd-Smith's idea consigned to the history books. The trams in this photograph belong to the time when 45 English Electric rail coaches with open sliding roofs were added to the fleet. Their moquette seats and twin windscreens, with a driver seated at the handle, were the height of luxury. Some 116 trams were purchased in this decade.

BIRD'S EYE VIEW

The view over rooftops picked out the Winter Gardens that were built in the 1870s. The complex provided indoor amusement and entertainment for the increasing number of tourists and visitors who had started to make Blackpool their holiday destination in ever increasing numbers. The company wanted to build an added attraction to rival Blackpool Tower that opened in 1894. It decided upon a gigantic wheel along the lines of the one that GW Ferris built for the 1893 Chicago Fair. A similar one had just been built for the 1895 Earls Court Exhibition in London. Blackpool's version had an axle of some 30 tons that rested on 8 columns set in 9 feet of concrete. The whole contraption weighed over 1,000 tons. The Auto Music Company was formed to operate the Big Wheel that turned for the first time in 1896. It cost just sixpence (2,5p) for a ride, half the price of the one in London. Blackpool has always given value for money! However, the venture was not a commercial success. One revolution took 15 minutes and each time one of its 30 cars reached the ground, the mechanism was stopped to allow another car full of people to be loaded. The wheel was dwarfed by the Tower, being less than half the height of its rival. Scrap metal dealers, Ward of Eccles, demolished the wheel in 1928 and Olympia Palace was built to replace it. The Winter Gardens themselves opened in 1878. There were grandiose ambitions that this would be a cultural centre, but they did not last long. By the following year, the star attraction was a girl being fired from a cannon. Despite its grand appearance, the acoustics were dodgy and the celebrated actress, Sarah Bernhardt, walked off stage at the end of the first act of her starring role in 'The Lady of the Camellias' and never returned.

At the start of the 20th century, rail was still king and steam its consort. This elevated view of Central Station shows how built up this part of town had become by that time. This was the period that was slap bang in the middle of the excursion boom that helped generate the economy that made our town the top resort in this land and in most of Europe as well, for that matter. However, it was the thousands of northerners who poured into the resort on a regular basis that made Blackpool a by-word for fun packed holiday amusement and relaxation. It was not cheap, with a ticket from Manchester costing three shillings (15p) for a male passenger. That was several days' pay for a labourer. Ironically and somewhat remarkably, women and children were both half price. The majority of trippers swept in by rail and those disembarking here were virtually on the seafront already. The first line into Talbot Road opened on 29 April 1846, with a second from Kirkham and Lytham terminating at Houndshill Station, as it was first known, from 6 April 1863. It did not become Blackpool Central until 15 years later. Despite becoming the main station, it closed on 1 November 1964 as part of the Beeching cuts. Part of the building was used as a bingo hall for a while, so it was not just cinemas that echoed to the call of 'clickety-click' in those days. This in turn was demolished in 1973 and Coral Island amusement centre built in its stead. After the opening of the M55 motorway in 1975, parts of the former railway line were remodelled as Yeadon Way, the link road to the car parks at the old railway sidings.

It is not often that you can see all three of Blackpool's piers in one photograph. Looking south in 1937 towards Lytham St Annes, out of picture, the distant South Pier is the newest of Blackpool's trio. Rather shockingly, considering the religious attitudes of our Victorian forefathers, the opening ceremony for the £50,000 addition to the resorts fun spots took place on Good Friday 1893. Two brass bands, an orchestra and choir were in attendance to mark the occasion. Considering that Sundays and holy days were taboo for frippery and fun, it seems remarkable that the event was allowed to take place. The Grand Pavilion opened in May that year. The Regal Pavilion was added in 1938, but this was replaced by the Beachcomber Amusement Arcade in 1963. Central Pier opened in 1868. As the coastline is fairly straight and flat, it was comparatively easy to build the pier right out into the sea at promenade level. Its first manager was Robert Bickerstaffe, the coxswain of the town lifeboat. North Pier was the first to see light of day when it was built in 1863 to a design by Eugenius Birch, the architect also responsible for piers at Margate, Bournemouth, Scarborough and many others. The Cenotaph, Blackpool's memorial to those who fell in wartime, can be seen close to this last pier. It was designed by Ernest Prestwich and sculpted from Cornish granite by Gilbert Ledward. It has a number of very handsome reliefs that include one that shows an unusual touch of realism, showing a German being trampled beneath the Tommies' feet. It was unveiled on 10 November 1923. Lest we forget.

With the Pleasure Beach and its roller coaster in the background, the Canberra flew impressively above the waves and away from its birthplace at Warton, just seven miles west of Preston. It was the first postwar aeroplane to be built there and soon developed a strong reputation for adaptability and reliability. It was a first generation jet engined light bomber, built by English Electric. Although it made the drawing board in May 1945, it was another four years before a prototype took to the skies. The first batch entered service with RAF 101 Squadron in 1951 and was an immediate success. Some 35 squadrons were eventually equipped with Canberras and valuable exports of the bomber

were made to places as far afield as Venezuela, Australia and South Africa. This was valuable export business in the austere postwar years. Even the Americans bought them, replacing their B-26 Invaders with B-57 Canberras. In 1957 a Canberra set a then world record for altitude flying when one model reached over 70,000 feet. Different generations of the aircraft continued in manufacture and service for well over half a century. The last ones flew photographic missions over Afghanistan in 2006. There are about 10 that are still airworthy, but their flying is restricted to appearances at air displays when their appearance is greeted with affection by those who have connections with the aeronautical industry.

Below: Blackpool would not be the same without its 42 acre Pleasure Beach. There can hardly be a soul in the land who has not set foot here at one time or another. As youngsters we used to thrill to the white knuckle rides, secure in the knowledge that the lad we were with would not let anything horrible happen to us. It did not stop us screaming at the top of our voices, however. Any girl wanting a more sedate time could stroll hand in hand with her beau as he showed off his skill with an air rifle, trying to win her a teddy bear. The sights on the gun were always faulty, if he was to be believed, but that did not matter. All that counted was that we were enjoying ourselves. How could we fail? Eddie Cochran songs and Freddie Cannon belting out 'Way down yonder' were just perfect, as was the sweet, sickly smell of the candy floss and the stale scent of fried onions. The initial park was founded by WG Bean in 1896 with the aim of making adults feel like children again. He succeeded.

Right: Clifton Drive, the A584, runs north from Lytham St Annes to Squires Gate where it becomes The Promenade on the start of its journey along the resort's sea front. In the centre of the picture we can make out Squires Gate Lane bridging the railway as it heads in from the direction of Great Marton Moss to join The Promenade just above where Pontin's now stands. This is one of the holiday camps that were founded by Fred Pontin (1906-2000), a Londoner from the East End who tried to rival Billy Butlin's empire. Pontin's Bluecoats were first seen at Burnham-on-Sea in 1946 and had initial success, but could never quite oust the Redcoats from their top spot in the affections of some British holidaymakers. The camp that we can see was set up in the summer of 1939, possibly as part of civil defence manoeuvres. The tents were pitched on land now used by Blackpool International Airport. In the distance, South Pier and part of the Pleasure Beach can be made out.

Above: You could park at the garage on Station Road, seen from above the entrance to South Pier, for just a shilling on 20 July 1948, according to the sign on the lamp standard. Woodhead's Café, on the corner of Simpson Street, was as good a place as any to get some light refreshment before facing the perils of the Pleasure Beach a hundred yards away to the right. Tony's Café on the front offered a more substantial repast with his traditional fish and chips, but those wanting to sample some stronger refreshment could always nip into the hotel on the right where a refreshing pint of Dutton's best mild would go down well. Thomas Dutton and son, William, established their brewery in the Salford district of Blackburn in 1799. In the late 19th century, the brewery was in the hands of the Tattersall family who were related to the Duttons by marriage.

Right: The Fylde peninsula runs for 13 miles from the Ribble estuary in the south to Morecambe Bay in the north. Lytham St Annes is a conurbation in the Fylde district. The neighbouring towns of Lytham and St-Annes-on-Sea have grown together and now form a seaside resort, sometimes seen as a smaller and more genteel alternative to nearby Blackpool.

This picture shows a stretch of land along the South Promenade, running parallel with Clifton Drive South, sweeping round the coastline past St Annes Pier.

By some standards the pier was a relatively modest affair, built to a length of 914ft (277m) at a cost of £18,000. It was opened by Lord Stanley on 15 June, 1885. In 1904 further, much more ornate work was carried out with the construction of a fabulous 1000 seater pavilion. The whole complex was finally completed in 1910 with the construction of the 'Floral Hall', which provided facilities for concerts, opera's and vaudeville acts. The pier facilities have played host to many famous performers including Gracie Fields, George Formby and Russ Conway. Several years after this picture was taken tragedy was to strike St Annes Pier when a serious fire completely destroyed the Pavilion. It was restored to some extent, but another fire on the pier in July 1982, destroyed it. About half the pier was then demolished to make the beach safe to use.

Like similar seaside resorts, St Annes in particular is a popular place to retire to, which has resulted in the average age of the population being higher than the national average. There are a considerable number of nursing and retirement homes, many located in former large houses along Clifton Drive, one of the main roads linking Lytham and St Annes.

There is some confusion, even among residents of the town, about whether the correct name is "St Annes" or "St Anne's". Although the name may originally have borne an apostrophe, it appears to have been dropped from the name by many of the residents of the town.

The sheds on the quayside at Fleetwood would have been overflowing with fish when this picture was taken in June 1949. This small port was one of the country's best known sources of the fruits of the sea. It was also well used as a steamer terminal, offering commercial and tourist links with Ireland, the Isle of Man and Scotland. About this time the fishing industry grew and became even more important to Fleetwood's economy, as the opening of the Manchester Ship Canal took away much of its cargo trade.

Clearly visible in this picture is Fleetwood Railway Station, on Queen's Terrace, which was on this site between 1883 -1966. Prior to this it was round to the left on Dock Street, opposite Church Street.

The Pharos Lighthouse, seen in the centre of this picture, is a 93-foot (28 m) tall sandstone lighthouse situated at the crossroads of Pharos Street and Lune Street. The lighthouse was designed in 1839 by Decimus Burton and Capt H.M. Denham. Construction was completed in 1840. Unusually for a functioning British lighthouse, it stands in the middle of a residential street. Though officially named the 'Upper Lighthouse', it has been known as the 'Pharos' since its construction, after the celebrated ancient lighthouse Pharos of Alexandria. The lighthouse was designed and constructed in conjunction with the much shorter (34 ft) Lower Lighthouse (also known as Beach Lighthouse) which stands on Fleetwood sea front. The lighthouses are designed to be used as a pair to guide shipping through the treacherous sandbanks of the Wyre estuary.

At the top right of this photo you can see the North Euston Hotel and Fleetwood Pier. The North Euston Hotel is another of Decimus Burton's designs, opening at enormous expense in 1841. The hotel derives its name from the time when there was no direct rail route from London to Scotland along the west coast. Travellers would have to alight at Fleetwood and take the sea ferry to Ardrossan and then travel by rail to Glasgow. The construction of the railway over Shap Fell in the Lake District in 1847 ended this sea/rail link.

Although never an elaborate structure the pier at Fleetwood holds a special place in history, as the last pier of its kind to be built in the UK. The 492ft (150m) opened on Whit Monday in 1910. By the time this picture was taken a small cinema had been added to the original pavilion on the wooden landing pier. Unfortunately in August 1952 a disastrous fire took place in the cinema, which could be seen 20 miles away. The pier was rebuilt almost immediately and was opened again the following year.

Left: The aeroplane was aimed across Blackpool towards the Tower in 1968. Below it, we can clearly see the dark shape of the redundant Central Station. Of course, Butcher Beeching, as the architect of the revamping of the nation's rail services in the 1960s was known, made sure that his axe fell far and wide. This part of the rail network was not spared and the place where once thousands of millworkers spilled across the platforms, anxious to blow their holiday pay during Wakes Weeks, fell silent in 1964, except for the shouts of the bingo caller. He left in 1973 and the land was cleared and redeveloped. Some new sea front amusement arcades were created, as were a new police station and multi-storey car park, with some residual spare land used as additional parking. The gasholder in the centre overlooked Borough Park, the former home to Blackpool's professional rugby league side. This site, sandwiched between Princess Street and Rigby Road, is now home to the Odeon Cinema. People with sharp eyes will just make out the top of a floodlight at the bottom left of the picture. This belongs to the Bloomfield Road stadium, home to Blackpool FC. The broad sweep of Central Drive comes up from the bottom, swinging left towards the Tower.

Below: In the mid 1960s it was not just the Oval cricket ground in Surrey that boasted a gasholder alongside its playing area. Blackpool Borough Rugby League Club once played its matches on Princess Street with a similar backdrop. The club entered the major league circles in 1954, using the Greyhound Stadium on St Annes Road as its home ground, although it borrowed the soccer stadium at Bloomfield Road for more prestigious matches. During its time at the dog track, Blackpool Borough never finished higher than 21st in the League. The club moved to this Borough Park site in 1963, playing and beating Salford in its inaugural game. Superstars Brian Bevan and Billy Boston both played for the club in the twilight of their careers, but they could not help lift Borough out of the second division. That had to wait until 1979, but success was short lived and relegation followed after one season with the big boys. The club went into liquidation in 1982, but managed to re-form and continue in the League. It had to leave Borough Park in 1987 as parts of the ground and its amenities were declared a safety risk. There then followed a nomadic period as the club reinvented itself as Springfield Borough in Wigan and then as Chorley Borough. By the end of the 1980s, it was playing in Altrincham as Trafford Borough.

MAKING A LIVING

In 1940, Warton Aerodrome on the Fylde was acquired to complement the RAF Coastal Command station at Squires Gate. Not long after the attack on Pearl Harbour in late 1941, it was decided to develop the site as a depot for the American Airforce and work was immediately begun on extending the runways and improving hangar facilities. Base Air Depot 2, as it was known to our guests, had as many as 20,000 personnel based there when it was operating at full capacity. The workforce was charged with getting new aircraft to battle readiness prior to their delivery to front line squadrons. Here we can see our allies assembling aero engines ready for fitting into anything from small fighter aircraft to large four engined bombers. The workshops and assembly lines were so busy that there could be as many as 300 planes waiting on the perimeter, ready to be flown to their new homes. After the war, Warton returned to RAF control before being taken over by English Electric in 1947. Since then it has been used by British Aerospace and its successor BAE as a testing station for such front line planes as the Canberra, Lightning, Tornado and Typhoon. The modern workforce claims still to be finding discarded chewing gum wrappers, Camel cigarette packets and Coca-Cola bottles.

Above: A dramatic scene dating from 1938. It features the construction work taking place to increase the car parking facilities in Blackpool which, in this instance, also provided a coach station below. The Talbot Road Bus Station with overhead multi-storey car-park was completed in 1939 and is remembered for its distinctive cream and green tiles. The cladding corresponded with the Corporation trams and buses and was considered to be very stylish in its day. It was therefore controversial when, in 1963, the cladding was replaced with grey corrugated steel.

Bottom left: Work is underway here, in 1955, on the site of what would become the location of British Home Stores. Prior to the construction work the area was used as an open-air market place with the adjacent Market Hall and Market Hotel. Car parking spaces were provided alongside the market area. The West Street multi-storey car park would more than compensate for the loss of parking spaces previously available, this structure went up at the same time as the British Home Store. The opening ceremony of BHS took in 1957.

Below: Even modern youngsters are familiar with enclosed police boxes, thanks to the continued success of Dr Who. They may be interested to know that there were also street telephones, like this one, where both bobbies and the general public could connect to the main police station switchboard. From there, the appropriate emergency service could be alerted. When an ordinary passer-by opened the door to this phone unit, a light was illuminated at headquarters, alerting staff to the equivalent of a 999 call. The officer, using this appliance on Talbot Square in 1956, could also be connected to various other police departments so that he could relay information to the most appropriate one. A more modern design of box was introduced in 1962, but this was phased out as more modern technology took over. They were also vandalised quite often. Blackpool's first, and initially only, policeman was a certain Constable Banks of the Lancashire Constabulary. He took up his post in 1850. The first police stations were built on Bonny Street and Abingdon Street. Blackpool Borough Police Force was not founded until 1887, with JC Derham as its first Chief Constable. A new HQ opened on South King Street on 5 June 1893 and served the town until its demolition in the 1970s. A new station was then built on Bonny Street.

Burton's Foods - Taking the Biscuit

The Company now called Burton's Foods Ltd was formed following the combination of the Horizon Biscuit Company Ltd and Burton's Gold Medal Biscuits in October 2000. It is owned by Duke Street Capital.

The Company is a leading branded and own-label supplier of quality biscuits and snacks, and is the number two branded player and second largest biscuit supplier in the UK.

It owns and bakes market-leading brands such as Maryland Cookies, Jammie Dodgers and Wagon Wheels, and bakes Cadbury's chocolate biscuits under licence.

Burton's has four bakeries around the UK: in Edinburgh, Moreton and Llantarnam as well as the Devonshire Road site in Blackpool.

But the Burton name has roots in Blackpool which go back much further in time than just to the year 2000.

The Blackpool Biscuit Company Ltd (later known as Bee Bee Biscuits) was first incorporated in 1922. Its founder was George F Burton, a local confectioner with shops in Blackpool, who also ran a School of Confectionery in Park Road. He had won Gold Medals for his famous Brandy Snaps which he had once sold on Blackpool Pleasure Beach.

Shareholders of the company formed in 1922 were local tradesmen who put up a total share capital of £12,500.

The first biscuit premises were a disused chapel where production continued through the early 1920s, before the Company extended to larger premises in Buchanan Street.

In the old premises there had been only a brick built Peel Oven, but in Buchanan Street they had installed a larger travelling-chain oven, though still very small by later standards.

By 1924 the Company was still making only a few lines of biscuits, amongst which were the very popular Ginger Nuts. It was a contract for the sale of these biscuits in quantity to Woolworths which now gave the company the resources needed to develop the business further.

That year the first traveller was taken on, as sales began to grow outside the Blackpool area. Distribution was at first only local, but gradually extended in Lancashire. As independent business built up, the Woolworth contract was phased out.

The name of the Company was changed in the mid-1920s to Bee Bee Biscuits Ltd, because it was suggested that people in Southport would not want to buy biscuits made in Blackpool!

Top left: *Founder, George F Burton.* **Left:** *Rolling out dough and cutting biscuits in the machine department in 1925.* **Above:** *The packing department in the 1920s.*

Bee Bee Biscuits, named after George Burton's twins, affectionately know as the Bonnie Bairns, developed, very quickly during these years, selling its biscuits in tins at a price of between 10d and one shilling per pound. These good quality biscuits undercut the price at which better known competitors were selling, and despite some serious competition from one firm selling inferior quality biscuits at just 6d per pound, they continued to thrive.

By the late 1920s it became obvious that the Company could not continue in its current premises. Flatts Mills at Walton-le-Dale was bought at a very low price and used in part for storage. Around the same time land at Devonshire Road was offered for sale, but more capital would be needed to build a new factory there.

It was at this point that Lesme Ltd, which had been selling the Biscuit Company small quantities of couverture, a high quality chocolate, began looking round to gain control of a small biscuit company in order to expand its sales of chocolate by the manufacture of half-coated chocolate biscuits, which were then becoming very popular.

Leslie H. Atwell, the Chairman and M.D. of Lesme Ltd, began negotiations with the Biscuit Company Directors. Final

agreement was reached in 1930/31 to purchase 51% of the shares for £40,000. Options were given to the existing Directors to leave the Company with compensation for loss of office providing they sold their remaining shares to the new holding company. Founder, George Burton, continued for a short period as Chairman before he also opted out and started a new biscuit Company which prospered and was eventually sold to the Weston Group.

In 1931 the Blackpool Company now became part of Lesme Ltd. The following year it did purchase the eight and a half acre site in Devonshire Road and building on the present site began. Meanwhile, the Company's registered office moved to London, but Blackpool continued to be the main manufacturing centre.

In 1933 it was envisaged that packaged biscuits would take over sales from biscuits being sold loose in the tin and orders were placed for American wrapping machinery. The Company became one of the first to introduce biscuits in air tight packing in this country.

Manufacture transferred to the new factory on its completion in 1934. A baking unit was installed in Lesme Buildings in Scrubbs

Top left: A brochure with a selection of Bee Bee products from Christmas 1937. *Above left:* The Bee Bee twins. *Above:* Bee Bee Bathing Belles welcome the Mayor and Mayoress to the factory in the early years. *Below:* The Bee Bee Biscuits factory in 1937.

Many of the younger male staff were called up to serve in the armed forces during the war, not returning to pick up the reins again until 1946. However, many of the wartime problems continued for many years. Rationing in the UK continued until 1952 and it was only about that time that 'zoning' for biscuits also came to an end. In 1947 the name of the Company was changed to Symbol Biscuits Limited and traded with an elephant as its logo with the ad tag of "an elephant never forgets", and who could forget Symbol Biscuits. Nine years later, in 1956, the introduction of Maryland and other cookie lines brought about a major advance in the Company's sales.

From the end of the war until the early 1960s the Company continued to expand both in distribution area and manufacturing capability, and also in the field of exports.

Lane where the full process of manufacture was started, including 'enrobing' or coating with chocolate.

Selling and distribution areas were extended both in the North and the Midlands as well as in the London area. Most of the development was financed by loans from Lyons, and as a result in 1938 Lyons bought out the whole of the shareholding and Bee Bee Biscuits became a wholly owned subsidiary.

Sales were extending rapidly throughout the United Kingdom but the Second World War temporarily put paid to any further expansion.

The outbreak of war in 1939 brought in official 'zoning', which meant a shrinking of the selling and distribution areas. But it also brought a considerable increase in the profits for the company, although a lot of these were drained off in high taxation.

Striking advances were not only made with the introduction of the now famous Maryland Cookies but also with its

Interestingly, although the Company had pioneered the packing of biscuits in packets as opposed to tins in 1933, on the outbreak of war, the packing of biscuits reverted to tins.

*Top left: The Packaging Department pose for a staff photograph in 1935. **Above left and right:** The number 4 oven (left) and a vertical mixer from 1940. **Below:** Symbol Biscuits Limited in the late 1940s.*

Private cars for representatives and executives totalled more than 100. On the accounts side the Company was dealing with some 20,000 customers and keeping 116 separate sales ledgers.

counterpart, Kentucky Cookie, and the delicious Gaytime Assorted. These and many other sweet, savoury and dry specialities moved off grocers' shelves into the homes of multitudes of consumers throughout the country and overseas.

On 2 April 1963, the Earl of Derby opened a further extension enabling the Company to increase production capacity, and a vigorous sales expansion took place both at home and overseas.

During the 1960s the Company opened a laboratory in Blackpool, along with a Marketing and Publicity Department as it also did a considerable amount of advertising.

By the mid-1960s it became obvious that the Company could not continue to trade in this way and remain profitable. The London factory was closed and all its plant and some of its staff moved to Blackpool.

On the 1 April 1968, Symbol Biscuits was fully integrated with Lyons Groceries Limited, a part of the J. Lyons Group of Companies based in

Top left: *A Symbol exhibition stand at the 1957 Manchester Food Trade Exhibition.* **Top right:** *A post war view of Symbol's typists at work.* **Left:** *The Viennese Whirls plant commissioned in 1976.* **Right:** *A Symbol 25 Club membership card. The club was set up for directors or employees who had completed 25 years of continuous service for the company. The object of the club was to promote good fellowship and the encouragement of the family spirit - a tradition of the company, to organise annual reunions and arrange other functions as desired.* **Below:** *Symbol Biscuits' float for the 1976 Blackpool Carnival parade.*

It was also in the mid 1960s that the Company began a long-standing connection with Sainsbury's, Tesco and other multiples, to supply them with biscuits in bulk. This would form the foundation of the Company's later successes.

Looking back it seems incredible that a production output which seldom exceeded 180 tons per week could support such a large organisation. At its peak this included Accounts, Costs, Sales, and other office staff of over 100 people. Sales representatives, including managers, also totalled around 100 people. There was also a distribution organisation with depots at Blackpool, London, Manchester, Liverpool, Wakefield and Birmingham. A fleet of delivery and depot feed vans totalled some 60 vehicles.

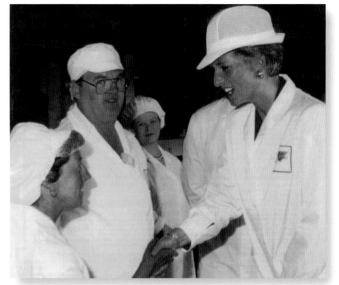

London and which were primarily engaged in the manufacture, distribution and sales of food products, catering and property in countries all over the world.

The Blackpool site was increased in 1970 by the purchase of 2.25 acres from British Rail which allowed further expansion. Symbol Biscuits now manufactured a wide variety of biscuits some sold in the well known Lyons' packs and some under customers' own label in stores and supermarkets throughout the United Kingdom. An ever-growing amount of products was also being exported to Europe and many other parts of the world.

All biscuits contain fat, flour and water, or other liquids, together with such materials as sugar, nuts, chocolate and, where appropriate, flavourings, colourings and other additives. It is the way that these are skillfully blended together that is the biscuit maker's art.

Each year the Company was using 13,000 tons of flours - 4,400 tons of fats and 3,400 tons of sugars. The six oven lines installed at the Blackpool factory were capable of producing up to 47 different kinds of biscuit - from cookies to cream crackers and shortcake to chocolate-coated digestives. The flexibility of production enabled them to bake in relatively short runs, so helping ensure that the biscuits would always be oven fresh on the shop shelf.

On 1 April 1973, Symbol Biscuits officially became Lyons Bakery Ltd, manufacturers of cakes and biscuits, whilst retaining the Symbol trade name.

The Smethwick (Birmingham) Factory of Lyons Bakery closed down in 1976. Its successful Viennese Whirls plant was transferred to Blackpool piece by piece and re-constructed on the site of the old No.2 Unit.

In 1977 the No.3 Unit was replaced by a brand new oven and wrapping machine set-up, as part of a programme to improve efficiency and increase production. By then 19,000 tons of biscuits were being produced annually. The biggest sellers were the well-known Maryland Cookies and Digestives, each accounting for 20% of total production.

A fully equipped laboratory staffed by skilful and experienced technicians checked the quality of all raw materials used in production. The same staff also carried out regular batch quality control checks on all finished products to ensure that they met customers' individual specifications.

A special test bakery enabled the Company to develop new recipes or products to meet individual customer requirements or changing market tastes.

Top left: Symbol Social Club's 1989 raft race. The Club began in 1929 as the Bee Bee Recreation Club. Top right: Staff meet and greet HRH Diana Princess of Wales, on her visit to the factory in 1991. Centre: Noel Edmonds grabs a handful of Maryland Cookies, which provided a tasty treat for children from the Airborne Trust on their visit to the factory in 1996. Far left and left: The Company's best selling Cadbury's Luxury Cookies and Maryland Cookies.

The factory also by now had its own fully equipped maintenance workshop. Staffed by skilled engineers, it kept the ovens baking and packing lines running by regular maintenance and in an emergency the workshop could, and did, manufacture in hours, spare parts which would normally take weeks from any other source.

The J. Lyons Group became part of Allied Breweries group of Companies in 1978 giving Symbol Biscuits its fourth controlling group since 1922. The next year saw the replacement of the old No.4 baking unit by the very latest in modern baking machinery, increasing productive potential even further.

Corporate changes continued when in 1981 Allied Breweries Limited became Allied Lyons. This was followed in 1983 by the Blackpool Company becoming a separate business entity from Lyons Bakery.

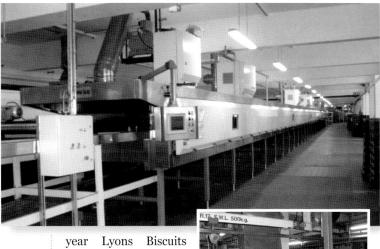

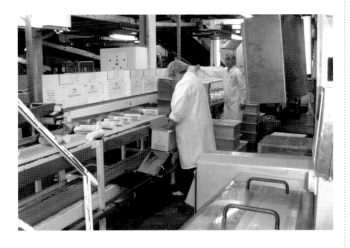

A new extension to house a new chocolate/baking/enrobing plant was built in 1984. The following year a new plant was commissioned – the first computer-controlled mixer with 'in-line' moulding, baking, cooling, enrobing and packaging equipment.

In 1987 a new caramel plant was installed to enable the Company to manufacture its own caramel topping. Twelve months later a third cookie plant was installed (No.7 plant) and a new staff amenities block was completed to house a new rest area, cloakrooms and toilets.

Symbol Biscuits became part of Lyons Bakeries (UK) Limited in 1990. It was now known as Lyons Bakeries (UK) Limited - Blackpool. A new No. 1 plant was commissioned to produce chocolate biscuits.

In 1993 large cookies were introduced on a new No.6 plant replacing the old cracker machine. That same

year Lyons Biscuits separated from Lyons Bakeries (UK) Limited and in 1994 the Company was acquired by Premier Biscuits, part of the Hillsdown Holdings Group.

In 1998 Premier Biscuits changed its name to The Horizon Biscuit Company Limited, which included two other sites, at Moreton and Harlow. This put the Company in a far stronger position within the biscuit industry.

Hicks, Muse, Tate & Furst acquired Burton's Biscuits in 2001, this gave the business five UK manufacturing sites and made it the second largest biscuit Company in Britain.

Following this event the Company changed its name to Burton's Foods Ltd – an ongoing reminder of Blackpool's own, George F Burton.

*Above left: Packing on Line 4. **Top right:** Two views inside the factory of the Line 5 oven (top) and Line 2 cutting machine (inset). **Below:** Burton's Foods' Devonshire Road, Blackpool premises.*

Partingtons Holiday Centres
Family Run Premier Parks in the North West

If it is a traditional, fun packed holiday you are seeking, set in delightful surroundings, then a Partingtons Holiday Centre is just the place for you. With three lively caravan parks in the Blackpool area and another in the more peaceful and pretty setting of North Yorkshire, there is plenty of choice on offer. Whether you are young or old, there is something for everyone both on site and close at hand.

If you enjoy the hustle and bustle of Britain's premier seaside town or strolling in the wonderful countryside, then a base provided by a Partington Centre is exactly what the doctor ordered. With over 60 years of experience in the business, the company knows what the great British public demands. An affordable holiday in a well appointed environment is delivered by a family firm who can provide that little bit extra in care and expertise when compared with the offerings of its competitors. People come first with Partingtons. It makes no excuses for not compromising on a quality service and it is no surprise that droves of happy customers come back year after year and are recognised by staff as old friends.

Windy Harbour and Newton Hall Holiday Parks are the longest established of the coastal centres. The former is the largest and offers new riverside and attractive lodge developments to augment its established customary static pitches. There is also plenty of room for tourers and those wishing to stay for a full season at a time. Newton Hall is well placed, not far from Stanley Park and Blackpool Zoo, and, as well as traditional caravanning services, can also offer a conference and meeting centre in its Country Club. Broadwater, just

Above: Founders, John William Partington Snr (left) Mary Partington (seated), Frank Partington (back centre), George Partington (right). *Below:* An early view of Windy Harbour office and camp entrance area.

the early years, there was just a wooden hut at the camp entrance serving as a grocer's shop and a shed halfway down the site selling newspapers. The main house doubled as an administration area.

The Partingtons ran the business as a family enterprise. As well as Frank, John and Mary had other children who were involved. John Jr, George and Mary Elizabeth all had parts to play and became shareholders as well. Both parents died during 1951, leaving the children to carry on the venture that was now called the Partington Property Company.

outside Fleetwood, was developed during the 1960s. With its outdoor bowling club, amusement arcade, sauna, invigorating spa pool and much, much more on offer, clients are never short of something to do.

Although Partington Hotels was founded on 13 November 1944, the holiday story actually began in the Great War. Frank Partington was one of the early band of Baden-Powell Boy Scouts and, as a lad, spent some time at a camp on the Isle of Man. There he saw German prisoners of war who were housed in caravans on one of the Manx estates. He recounted what he had seen to his father, John William Partington, and the germ of an idea was sown. John was originally a corn miller in Manchester and, in company with his wife Mary, also owned several Blackpool hotels, as well as Newton Hall House and its lands at Staining. During the last war, many soldiers were billeted in these premises.

It was around this time that Frank reminded his father of his experiences on the Isle of Man over a quarter of a century earlier and persuaded him to open part of the family grounds to caravans. The first one arrived at Newton Hall in 1948. In

Top left, above and below: Three more early views of the Partingtons Holiday Centres at Newton Hall (top left), Ballyferris, Northern Ireland (above) and Broadwater (below).

sometimes the trees won the battle! He was also a hard worker, doing a daytime shift on the park and frying fish in the evenings.

In May 1960, John and Mary Elizabeth, or 'Bessie' as everyone knew her, sold out to their brothers, leaving Frank and George to fly the family flag on their own. In that same year, they bought Broadwater Caravan Park. Then, in 1964, they acquired Ballyferris Caravan Park in Northern Ireland, which was later sold in the 1970s. Frank was the entrepreneurial one, having left school at 15 and setting up a successful mattress manufacturing company in Staining Windmill. He

As new buildings were erected so the Newton Hall site developed during the 1950s, the Partingtons decided to expand their holdings and, in 1954, purchased Windy Harbour Farm. This was an established centre where locals came for afternoon tea and coach parties called while taking passengers on mystery tours. George moved into the old farmhouse with his wife and young daughters in order to develop the grounds as a caravan park. Their home doubled as the clubhouse, opening as such in 1956. Initially, there was no mains electricity and they had to rely on a generator. This had a habit of running out of fuel at awkward times and George sometimes had to fill it with diesel and pump it up by hand so that a bingo session could be completed. He was something of a character, sitting at the pianola and taking a bow while it still played. His family also recall him pulling down trees, using a single decker bus as a tractor, though

took charge of running the offices, whilst George took control of developing the Parks. Even so, the brothers needed more help as the business was now expanding on several fronts. Trevor Kearsley, George's future son-in-law, joined the company in 1964 to develop and manage the latest acquisition.

stuck. The more he tried to dig himself out, the more the machine got into trouble. Eventually, everything caved in on man and machine and it took three tractors to effect the rescue. This was a case of going in at the deep end!

Sadly, Frank died in 1969, aged just 62. He had helped lay the solid foundations for the best of companies and it continued to grow after his death, thanks in no little part to his initial vision and subsequent skills.

Tarn Caravan Park near Skipton was purchased in 1974, with Tarn House Hotel being acquired in 2003. The 17th century inn provides a lovely backdrop to a quiet and picturesque part of the world that is the gateway to the Yorkshire Dales.

Partingtons has never rested on its laurels. Yet, while constantly striving to keep abreast of modern developments, its main focus has always been on customer satisfaction. It carries on looking to add to what it can offer.

Top left, facing page: The entrance area at Newton Hall. Centre right, facing page: Floating boats in a puddle at Newton Hall in the late 1950s. Bottom, facing page: A north east view of Windy Harbour in the 1960s. Top: The old playground at Windy Harbour. Left: Windy Harbour Club. On the left is George Partington. Below: Having fun at Broadwater in 1973.

Broadwater Club opened in 1966. Even though it was not fully completed, customers on the park wanted refreshment and entertainment. They did not mind that the lights had no shades or that the bar was a temporary structure. They happily played bingo in the aisles, resting their cards on each other's backs as the place was so busy. Trevor later became the General Manager and a director of the company. As well as becoming relatives when Trevor married George's daughter, Christine, the two men were good friends and got into a few scrapes together. On one memorable occasion they were excavating for the swimming pool at Newton Hall when George and his bulldozer got

In 1983, buildings and land alongside Newton Hall were bought from the Blackpool Tower Company. One such building, the former Queens Brewery for Catterall and Swarbrick, known locally as 'come and sup' from the brewers' initials, had also been used as a laundry, garage and storage area. In 1997, it was converted into a children's facility, called Grunty's Fun Factory. It took its name from Andrea's mispronunciation of 'grumpy', which Christine had used when referring to her grandfather. Needless to say, George was highly amused.

In 2004, it became a nursery. Another building, formerly used to house and train circus animals, has become the biggest bowling centre in the county. The bowling club has won national and all England titles consistently over the last few years.

There was a major fire at the Newton Hall clubhouse and offices in 2004. An extensive rebuild was opened by the Mayor of Fylde in 2006. The necessary new premises at least gave Partingtons the chance to continue with its modernisation programme, particularly in the field of information technology. Initially, when computers were introduced in the mid 1990s, people were suspicious of them. Despite some resistance from those who liked the 'old ways' and regarded a disk drive as something only useful as a door stop, Andrea and Robert eventually succeeded in getting the whole company computerised. Guests now even have the benefit of free wi-fi in the caravans and lodges on the Blackpool sites.

Top left: Newton Hall, rebuilt after the devastating fire in 2004, pictured inset. *Top right:* Mr Trevor A Kearsley (right) pictured at Partingtons' Bowling Centre with former World Bowls Champion, David Bryant CBE (left) and Eric Bennett (centre). *Bottom left:* 2007 Egham Trophy winners - members of the Partingtons national and all England title winning bowls club. *Left, from left to right:* Martin Beardsworth, George Kemp and Robert Kearsley receive the 2009/2010 Highly Commended Caravan Holiday Park and Holiday Village Award, for Windy Harbour. *Below:* Andrea Challis and Darren Chambers receive the winners award as Newton Hall is named Caravan Holiday Park of the Year 2008/2009.

Partingtons is a company with a friendly face that has looked after its workforce as well as its clients. Some employees seem to

have been there forever. Derek and Doreen Aston honeymooned at Windy Harbour and stayed on to work there, later being promoted to Club Managers and remaining for a further 44 years. Brian Maycock met Hillary, his future wife, whilst she was on holiday at Windy Harbour, he became Assistant General Manager whilst they ran Windy Harbour as a team. They have now worked for the company for a total of 88 years between them. Vina Bateman helped to build the company for 27 years as Sales Manager and David Skelton, Joe Scott, Colin Baker and Steve Linacre are all still going strong with 30-plus years behind each of them.

The firm is still a family concern, though George Partington died at the grand old age of 91 in 2007. He had served his town as a JP and Chairman of the Bench, but will be best remembered for his work on the parks and for driving a JCB well into his late 80s. His wife, Margaret, a former company director, died the following year.

Freda Partington, Christine Kearsley and Judy Brown (nee Partington) are other members of the family involved at

directorial level and the business now has its fourth generation in charge of running it. Trevor and Christine's children, Robert Kearsley and Andrea Challis have both risen through the ranks and are the current driving forces.

Sixty years ago you had a pitch in a field with no amenities. The first static caravans were the size of today's tourers and had no access to drains, mains electricity, toilets or showers. Back then, you got a new caravan for about £250. For an average price today, add a couple of noughts at the end. Some things, though, do not change. Partington Parks provide satisfaction and customers feel as if they have been treated with courtesy and afforded the respect that helps create the happy atmosphere of a wonderful holiday that will never be forgotten. Why else would many people decide to buy a caravan at one of these parks rather than rent? The answer is simple. They want to keep on returning.

Top left: Newton Hall's new club. *Left:* The new swimming pool at Windy Harbour. *Above:* Bowling at Broadwater Caravan Park. *Below:* Tarn House Caravan Park and Country Inn, built in 1650 as a Manor House in the heart of the North Yorkshire Dales.

Beaverbrooks the Jewellers
A Truly Sparkling Business

We all know that the Lancashire coast is one of the finest places to live in the whole of England. But it is also one of the best places to work: and that's official! According to a Sunday Times employee survey St Annes-based Beaverbrooks the Jewellers is the best company to work for in the whole of Britain.

For some readers Beaverbrooks may just bring to mind the jewellery store in Blackpool's Church Street. But Beaverbrooks is much more than just one store.

In fact Beaverbrooks is one the country's most prestigious firms with 65 branches nationwide.

In 2009 the company celebrated its 90th anniversary.

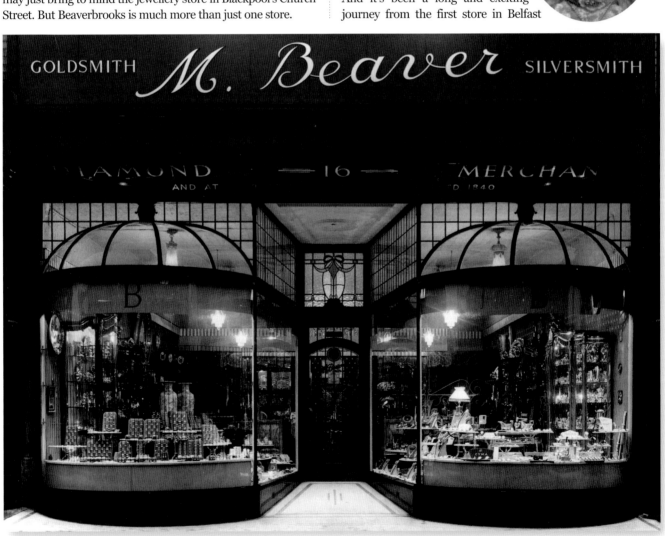

This very special business famous for selling gorgeous jewels started out when its original founders, brothers Isaac, Maurice and Harry Adlestone, set up their own shop. Beaverbrooks is still owned by direct descendants of its founders. And it's been a long and exciting journey from the first store in Belfast

was where 'Adlestones' was first registered as a company. The office moved to Shudehill in Manchester in 1931. The 1930s were a period of growth for the company. A store was opened in Huddersfield and another opened in Oldham Street, Manchester in 1935. The Beaverbrooks name first appeared above the company's Oldham Street store.

In Blackpool the firm traded as J Payne & Sons and Harland's. The first store on the Fylde coast opened before the second world war, though in those days opening only during the holiday season before becoming a permanent fixture trading all year round.

All the shops had different names and the Adlestone brothers were looking for a single name to trade under.

which opened in 1919, right up to a brand new, dazzling store which opened at the end of 2008 in Westfield, London.

Over the years Beaverbrooks has grown into an award winning success story, with 65 branches nationwide, and recognition as the very best place to work. The strong sense of 'family' that runs throughout the company means everyone who works for the firm shares in its success and can celebrate its continuing philosophy of enriching lives for both customers and staff.

It was back in 1910 when the three Adlestone brothers, Isaac, Maurice and Harry took to the streets with no more than suitcases full of silverware, loads of ambition and a vast amount of enthusiasm.

Though born in Britain the brothers' family's roots were in Russia. Boot maker David Adlestone and his wife Barbara had arrived in Britain only in 1880.

In 1919 in Belfast the brothers opened their first store selling giftware of every kind. Only later would they specialise in jewellery. Another stalwart of the business, Jack Silverstone, also now joined the Adlestone brothers; he would work for the firm until his death in 1962.

By 1920 an office was opened in Manchester in Swan Street as the brothers saw more opportunity to grow their business. This

Beaverbrooks was chosen as the corporate name after Lord Beaverbrook, at that time a well known and admired public figure, whose name was synonymous with honesty and integrity.

*Top left and top right, facing page: David and Betty Adlestone. **Left and above:** Early exterior and interior views of the company's M. Beaver store in St. Annes on Sea, opened in 1946. **Right:** Private rooms for customer viewing in the 1960s.*

Within the company this name became a great debating point because the long name was challenging to fit above some shop fronts: each brother denied that it was ever his idea! An additional problem was encountered when Lord Beaverbrook began to get correspondence, some complementary, but a few very much otherwise, intended for Beaverbrooks the Jewellers.

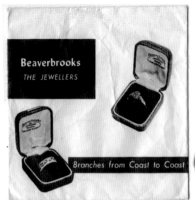

The office moved to St Annes Road West, in St Annes in 1940. The reason for the move to St Annes was wartime evacuation: the office in Shudehill, Manchester was 'bombed out'. It was hardly the best of times. Following the outbreak of war in 1939 many staff were called up for service in the armed forces, at the same time the inevitable shortage of gold whilst hostilities lasted caused the company to close stores and in addition to such problems every company was taxed at 100% of profits above a certain level in order to fund the war effort. Many staff had second jobs, such as air raid wardens, and Beaverbrooks

partnered with one of their suppliers to develop a munitions factory.

A shop opened in St Annes in 1946, trading as M Beaver Jewellers, the name of the firm's upmarket shop in Manchester. The three Adlestone brothers and their two nephews Sydney and Percy Brown combined

their businesses in 1948. Percy Brown, who was trading as Mawby & Neal in Bradford, and Sydney Brown, trading as Sydney Brown in Ashton, had been buying wholesale from the Adlestone brothers. They were brought into the business at this time because two of the Adlestone brothers were in poor health. Maurice Adlestone would die in 1952, Isaac and Harry both died in 1955.

By then 17 stores were under the company umbrella in Liverpool, Blackpool, Manchester, Huddersfield and Bradford. Over the next four years Beaverbrooks stores would also open in Birmingham and Glasgow.

Isaac Adlestone's son Gerald would be the second generation of the Adlestone family to join the firm. Sydney Brown would be followed into the business by his son Michael and Percy Brown was followed by his son Andrew.

Today the latest generation to be actively part of the Beaverbrooks' family tree are Michael Brown's son Daniel and Gerald Adlestone's son Mark.

The firm moved its offices to Adele House in Park Road, St Annes in 1982. By that time Beaverbrooks stores had opened all over the North of England and in Glasgow. The North West was very much their heartland with 3 stores in Blackpool, 4 in Manchester and 2 in Liverpool. There was however, no shop further south than Leicester.

The St Annes store closed in 1997 but elsewhere growth has continued. And with good reason.

Go into any Beaverbrooks shop today and you'll leave with an extra bit of sparkle in your life. And it's not just down to the dazzling jewellery.

By offering the weary shopper a cup of tea, a comfortable seat, a few minutes of chat and detailed advice about the products on offer, the company's 800 staff are doing all they can to boost the buying experience, and put a smile on the face of shoppers.

"It's about the difference we can make to their day. If someone comes into the shop in a bad mood, that doesn't mean they have to leave in a bad mood," according to Beaverbrooks' managers. "Our main focus is always making our customer happy. It is all about enriching their lives. It's not forced or false. It's genuinely what we want to do here." It is also what Mark Adlestone, managing director of the Lytham St Anne's-based jewellery chain, who joined the firm in 1978, wants to do for his colleagues. "Consultative paternalism is how I describe the way we run the business," he says. "We look after people as if we were a family. We really do listen to our people."

Beaverbrooks staff are the most content in the country, according to the Sunday Times topping the newspaper's annual rankings of the '100 Best Companies to Work For' in 2009 and always in the top four since they started entering them in 2004.

Beaverbrooks staff don't believe that profit is the only thing driving the company and feel that managers care about them as individuals.

Top left, facing page: Early packaging. Left: Beaverbrooks, Bank Hey Street, Blackpool pictured in the 1950s. Above: Beaverbrooks, Church Street, Liverpool in the 1960s.

"Sometimes you end up selling something less valuable in monetary terms, but it's more suited to the customer's needs," says one retail sales associate. "Money is important, but it's not the only reason we are here. Ethics are one of the main things which drive this company."

Training focuses on developing every aspect of the employee. Staff feel the job is of great personal benefit to them and is good for their personal growth.

"The person you are outside work is the person you are in work. The behaviours you exhibit are the same," says Mark Adlestone. This approach gives staff transferable life skills, instead of job-specific training. "It's a powerful thing that goes beyond making them better salespeople. People aren't machines. Everything has a knock-on effect and we recognise that."

This ethos lies at the heart of Beaverbrooks, and is communicated from the day someone joins the organisation.

People feel a strong sense of family in their teams, and managers care about their job satisfaction. Beaverbrooks' ethics extend further than customers and staff - the workforce is confident that the firm's support of worthy causes is not driven by a desire for good publicity.

The Beaverbrooks' philosophy is about how we spend our time in life, the memories we create of fun and laughter, of shared successes, of overcoming challenges and of caring for others. It is about learning new skills, challenging ourselves to do more, and making those dreams happen. It's the things that enrich us.

Today the company and all its people are very proud to be known on the high street and in the business world, for integrity, passion and a caring approach. Over 800 people in 66 locations throughout the United Kingdom - with thirteen stores in the North West region alone - not to mention internet and mail order teams, are all working hard at 'Making it Special' for customers and staff, by creating wonderful experiences which in turn enrich peoples' lives.

Direct descendants of the founders, the fourth and fifth generations of the Brown and Adlestone families, are still the

*Top: Advertising from 1960s. **Left:** Beaverbrooks, Church Street, Blackpool in the 1980s. **Below:** Beaverbrooks annual 10K Fun Run.*

custodians of Beaverbrooks. Still family-owned, it remains one big family.

The company cares about its people and Beaverbrooks' people care about others. Staff help in their communities by giving their time to local organisations, charities and schools. The company is able to support its people even more in this way by giving them time to spend with people who need help within their normal working hours.

Beaverbrooks actively encourages its teams to take part in fundraising activities and sponsored events and matches any money staff raise for registered charities. In 2008 for example staff raised a fantastic £31,648 which the company matched together raising £63,296.

Every year, the company gives 20% of its post-tax profits to charity, and staff choose which causes to support. During 2008 alone it gave £756,000 to charities both in the UK and overseas. Since 2000 Beaverbrooks has donated over £4 million to charity.

An annual event since 1982, the Beaverbrooks Blackpool 10K Fun Run has raised over £1,000,000 for local charities. Each year thousands of runners transform Blackpool's Golden Mile into a sea of colour, from serious road racers to fancy dress gorillas, each person raising money for a worthy charity.

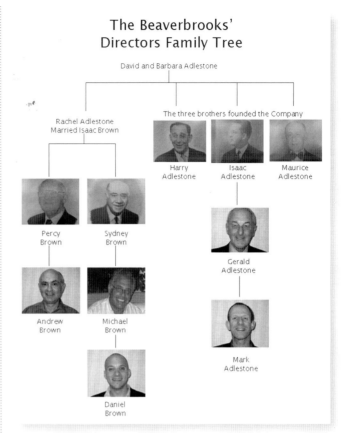

The Beaverbrooks'
Directors Family Tree

event. The Bike Ride has raised over £150,000 for Brian House Childrens' Hospice.

Today everyone who works for Beaverbrooks is proud to be associated with this award-winning firm. And Blackpool and St Annes are equally proud to be home to this truly sparkling business.

Top: The Beaverbrooks' Directors family tree. **Left and below:** *Just two of the 60 plus Beaverbrooks stores today: Belfast (left), where it all began and Blackpool, Church Street.*

Starting and finishing at the Hilton Hotel, the route runs along Blackpool's famous promenade.

The 2009 run was in support of Cancer Research UK. Cancer Research UK is the world's leading independent organisation dedicated to cancer research.

Another local event is the Beaverbrooks Bike Ride which first took place in 1992 with 180 riders taking part. Since the first Bike Ride the event has grown and grown with just over 700 people taking part in last year's

Clifton Quality Meats Ltd
Two Family Firms, One Great Name

Today's Clifton Quality Meats Ltd is a collaboration between two family butchery businesses. Its dual roots go back over a century. At first a purveyor of fine meat, poultry and game only along the Fylde coast, sales are now nationwide.

Kens Meat Market was founded in 1973 and became 'KMM Catering Ltd' in 1980 trading from St Albans Road, St Annes, and Cheltenham Road, Blackpool. In 1996 the firm became Clifton Quality Meats Ltd following relocation to state-of-the-art premises in Blackpool's Cornford Road.

The history of the present day company, however, goes back much further than 1973: in 2002 'CQM' merged with R. Benson Catering Meats Ltd with a history of its own dating back to the early 1900s.

Kens Meat Market was founded by Kenneth Hellewell. Ken was born in Ryhill, a mining village near Barnsley, in South Yorkshire. He had started work there at the village butcher's shop which also had a slaughterhouse at the rear.

Already an experienced butcher by the time he came to Blackpool, Ken worked at Binns Butchers in Fleetwood and was later Butchery Manager at the Blackpool Co-op before opening his own business, Kens Meat Market at 132, St Albans Road, St Annes.

Ken and his wife Sandra opened the shop with just one part-time employee. The business soon expanded to supplying catering firms, thereby employing further staff, including Ted Cottam, during his first spell with Ken.

Above: *Kenneth Hellewell, founder of Kens Meat Market.*
Below: *An early exhibition of Kens Meat Market.*

By the late 1980s Ken was also leasing a cold store and factory on the site of Blackpool Abattoir. It was there that a meat cutting and packaging operation was carried out for Iceland Frozen Foods.

Ken's pursuit of all year round business would lead to an increase in out-of-town trade run from St Albans Road, leaving the Blackpool hotels to be serviced from Cheltenham Road.

The increase in out-of-town business and the increasingly demanding Health and Safety and Food Regulations led to the need for larger premises. As a result the Cornford Road premises were acquired in 1996, along with a new company name.

The growth in the business had been the result of the efforts of many people, both colleagues and family members. Ken's wife Sandra had worked at the shop in St Albans Road and at home on the paperwork. His brother Colin, who had an HGV license, drove the containers of meat to the Iceland Frozen Food depot at Deeside. Brother–in–law Michael Storey was a butcher at various sites and worked at the Blackpool Abattoir site too, as did Ken's sister Brenda and Colin's wife Dorothy. Ken's son Jon worked in various roles in the 1990s, mainly as a butcher. Ken's niece Julie worked in the office at St Albans Road and his nephew Stephen started as a Saturday boy whilst still at school, as did his son Daniel in the late 1990s.

In the 1970s Blackpool hotels were busy from Easter to the end of October. From then until the Spring, however, business was slack. In the quieter months Ken sliced bacon for businesses in Liverpool. Always looking for all year round business and seeing that there might be an opportunities for growth in that line of business, he opened a bacon factory in St Heliers Road, Blackpool. It soon became apparent, however, that a very large amount of capital investment was needed for equipment. Ken decided that what capital he had would be better invested in what he knew best: the meat business.

Howard Chant joined Ken in 1976 and was the accountant for the company until Ken moved to Ireland in 1996. Howard then became Managing Director of the company and continued until he retired in 2006.

In the early 1980s Ken acquired the Louis Edwards depot at 3, Cheltenham Road, in Blackpool. At the time the depot was used to deliver meat to schools across the North of England. Further butchers' shops were acquired in Cleveleys, Layton and a second shop in St Annes.

Top left: Kens Meat Market 132, St Albans Road, St Annes.
Above left: Skilled butchers at work. Below: Left to right: Bill Wyllie, Peter Costello, Stephen Hellewell, Bill Holmes and Stephen Riches.

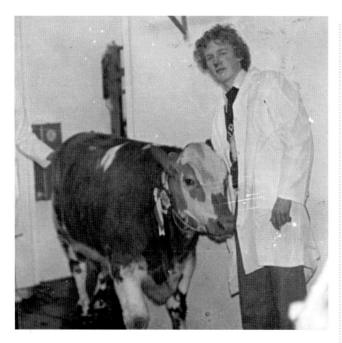

James Smith joined the company in the late 1970s as a sales representative. He was responsible for a large increase in sales to the Blackpool area. He worked hard not only to maintain but to increase that business. It was James Smith who started 'Caterama', usually held six weeks before Easter, where the company re-established contact with the previous season's hoteliers and reconfirmed business for the new season.

Stephen Lawton joined the company at Cornford Road in the late 1990s. What was needed to make full use of the large factory was more sales. Steve achieved this, and more importantly it was all-year-round business. Steve introduced some big name customers, providing the company with a much larger profile and helping it become one of the largest catering butchers in the North of England.

After his stint as a Saturday boy Stephen Hellewell was at first a shop butcher but he later moved into the rear at St Albans Road to work with Ken and learn the catering side of the business. Stephen took over as Factory Manager in the late 1990s at Cornford Road. His initial reorganisation of the factory, particularly the shift system the butchers were working, made for a far better working environment.

Over the years, under the leadership of Howard Chant, the backing of Ken and Stephen's buying, costing expertise and forward thinking, the company was able to progress to a new level.

In January 2002 a dramatic event occurred with the merger of Clifton Quality Meats with the long established firm of R Benson Catering Meats Ltd. The business that became, first R Benson & Sons, and later R Benson Catering Meats Ltd, had begun life in 1904 started in Kirkham by Richard Benson, who had a butcher's shop with a slaughterhouse at the rear. He bought beef, lamb and pork from local farmers and at livestock auctions. His sons Jack, Tom and Albert carried on the business followed by a third generation Richard and John Benson.

Under the regime of Richard and John a shop was opened in Blackpool in 1973 and another in Lytham in 1980. The focus was still mainly on retail sales, however, with some local accounts with restaurants. By the early 1980s the fourth generation, Stephen and Michael Benson, were becoming more active in the running of the business.

The firm's own slaughterhouse had closed in the late 1990s due to ever more onerous EU Regulations. At around the same time a supermarket had opened in Kirkham which greatly reduced

Top left: *Stephen Benson with a prize-winning beef animal. Bensons regularly purchased the prize-winner of a local livestock auction in the late 70s.* ***Above and left:*** *Interior and exterior views of R. Benson & Sons' Kirkham shop.*

local trade. It was clearly time to move into the catering side of the meat business.

In 1999 Simon Rigby, a local farmer and businessman with connections to the Benson family, along with Stephen and Michael Benson, formed a new limited company R. Benson Catering Meats Ltd.

The firm, with Managing Director Michael being instrumental, soon acquired a considerable amount of hospital and County Council business alongside other contracts for meat supplies.

Shortly afterwards Bensons purchased Binns of Fleetwood, Ken Hellewell's former employer for nearly 30 years.

In January 2002 Simon Rigby bought Clifton Quality Meats from Ken Hellewell and merged the two companies The merged company expanded from its Blackpool base in 2003 to include a purpose built unit in Leeds. Its delivery areas are now expanding from the North West to the borders of Scotland and down to the Home Counties, across from Wales to Humberside.

In 2006 Stephen Hellewell became Managing Director, Stephen Riches was promoted to Factory Manager after over 20 years of service and Stephen Benson was appointed Finance Manager.

Clifton Quality Meats launched its own branded products in 2007, Northern Gold Beef and Northern Gold Lamb. In 2009 Clifton Quality Meats purchased a new state-of-the-art facility in Normanton, West Yorkshire, to replace the existing unit in Leeds.

The company now has over of 60 employees across its sites. All management are qualified to a minimum NVQ Level 3 and all other staff to a minimum of NVQ Level 2.

Today, under the leadership of Simon Rigby, whose family have been farmers for over 100 years, the company continues to emphasise family values, highlighted by the fact that Stephen Hellewell's son Daniel, his wife Maureen and step-daughter Alison all play a part in the day-to-day running of the business, thus promoting those same family values that have been at the forefront of its growth for so many years.

Top: Stephen Hellewell (left) and Stephen Benson alongside one of the company vehicles. **Centre:** The company's own brand, Northern Gold Beef and Northern Gold Lamb, launched in 2007. **Left:** Simon Rigby, owner of Clifton Quality Meats.

Arnold School - Honour, Virtue and Excellence.

Blackpool's Arnold School has some very distinguished former pupils. Among those who have attended this mixed, independent day school are the England batsman Tom Graveney, Sir William Lyons, founder of Jaguar cars, Dr. Michael Smith, who received the Nobel Prize for Chemistry in 1993, and Chris Lowe, lead singer of The Pet Shop Boys. Other notable ex-pupils include David Ball (of pop group 'Soft Cell'), Peter Purves (TV personality) Michelle Walton (Opera Singer) and Jonas Armstrong (actor). James Armfield OBE DL (43 caps for England Soccer, 15 as captain) is a former pupil and is presently Vice Chairman of Governors.

Today's school was founded by Frank Truswell Pennington in 1896. Known initially as South Shore Collegiate School, it moved to its present site in Lytham Road when Pennington took over and gradually expanded the buildings of an earlier school. Pennington adopted the former school's name of Arnold House School, named after the famous Dr Thomas Arnold, one-time Headmaster of Rugby School. The original Arnold House School had been set up by a Thomas Ward who had come to Blackpool from Leeds in 1868 and who was associated with the Wesleyan Methodist Movement. The name was later shortened to Arnold School.

In 1903, William Henry Denham, the first boy on the school register in 1896, organised a football match between the school and the Headmaster suggested the match be made an annual event. Twenty seven of the old boys met the following year and formed an Association of Arnold House Old Boys.

Before his death in 1938, Pennington gave the school to the Old Boys who elected a Governing Council. From its inception, Arnold has attracted pupils of the highest calibre from the Fylde coast. In return, the school has given Lancashire many of its most distinguished citizens.

The Junior School was opened in 1920 in Horncliffe Road. On the first morning of term 52 boys assembled. A separate preparatory form was also instituted and there was a kindergarten department in the mornings for children under seven.

Top left: Founder, Frank Truswell Pennington. *Top right:* An early view of the School on Lytham Road. *Centre:* The Arnold School crest. *Left:* A garden party, a regular occurrence in the early years of the school. *Above:* An awards ceremony dating from the late 1890s.

Successive headmasters built on the solid foundations provided by F T Pennington. His immediate successor, Frank Holdgate, established his own reputation as well as pushing Arnold forward into a new age. Cameron Cochrane, (headmaster 1973-1979) took the decisive step towards co-education. Cameron Cochrane was succeeded by Richard DW Rhodes (1979-1987), John AB Kelsall (1987-1993) and William T Gillen (1993-2003).

Under today's headmaster, Barry M Hughes, the school's record of excellence has led to national and international recognition.

The school has made a steady investment in new buildings. Developments in the 1990s included new Art and Music Departments, All-Weather Facilities, a state-of-the-art Design and Technology Centre and a new Kindergarten Department taking boys and girls from the age of two.

The importance of sport and games is reflected in the creation of the Sports Hall, complete with climbing wall, fitness suite and changing rooms. Also in 1998 interest in music and drama was further stimulated by the opening of a drama studio.

Junior School buildings (for children from 4 to 11 years of age) were extensively remodelled and modernised in 2003.

The Lawrence House Music Centre, which includes a large recital area and recording studio, was opened by Chris Lowe in 2006. Improvements to the Kindergarten have continued. The premises can now boast improved and enlarged indoor and outdoor play areas.

The use of computer technology is evident in the quality of the specialist ICT rooms and in the recent investment in interactive ICT in every classroom.

In 2008 Arnold School became a member of the United Church Schools Trust, an independent Christian educational charity that manages a number of independent schools and maintained academies throughout the country.

Throughout over a century of service the school has retained its Latin motto 'Honor Virtutis Praemium' and remains true to that assertion: honour is still the reward of virtue. Arnold School is delighted to proclaim that it has 'a proud past and a bright future'. The Good Schools Guide rightly describes it as 'A lovely school where the hard work ethic doesn't overwhelm the pleasure of learning and growing up'.

Top left: Arnold School's Kindergarten Department. Top right: The impressive all-weather sporting facilities. Centre: The pleasure of learning at Arnold School. Below: A 2009 view inside the school grounds.

Fylde Floor Co. Ltd - Carpeting Blackpool

The Fylde Floor Co. Ltd, as it is today, was established 1949. Its founder was Wilfred Shillito, who had previously been employed at Firth Carpets, in Brighouse, near Halifax, from 1919 until 1947.

Made redundant, Wilfred moved to Blackpool to open a guest house, which turned out to be a disaster, due to his wife's ill health.

In 1949 Wilfred borrowed £494 to buy a small corner shop on Central Drive called Fylde Floor Co.. The shop sold linoleum, rubber floors, coconut matting and plastic. Not a carpet in sight.

Next door was a ladies hairdresser and on the opposite side of the road a newsagents, an ironmongers, a greengrocers, a shoe shop, a fish and chip shop and a confectioners. There was also a drapers shop run by a mother and her two daughters who took bets as a sideline. A sweet and tobacco shop completed quite a cosmopolitan group of retail outlets.

The corner premises at 304 Central Drive, which are the location of the store today, belonged to Alf Cooke, who sold fireplaces in one part of the building and had a wholesale rock and fancy goods business in the other.

Wilfred's son Alfred had been working in the insurance business in Leeds before the move to Blackpool. The new family business provided him with what he called 'an Irishman's rise' - more responsibility for less money.

Top left: Alfred Shillito. ***Above and below:*** *Interior and exterior views of the Fylde Floor Co. premises in 1986.*

Having experience in book-keeping, Alfred's first job was to get the books in order: Wilfred was a good businessman but not too keen on the paperwork and bookkeeping.

In lieu of a pension from his previous employers, Wilfred was allowed an allocation of carpets worth £500 per month, supplemented by a further £250 per month from a connection he had established with the firm of Cooke & Sons Co. Ltd, a subsidiary of B.M.K. Carpets. This provided a worthwhile foundation from which to launch the business.

There were very few fitted carpets in those days as carpets had just come off rationing, so Wilfred took his allocation of carpets in carpet squares and rugs. The allocation of carpets arrived the first week of the month, and following a small advert in the local Gazette they were all sold within a week. Goods were often 'seconds' or even 'thirds', but a strategically placed chair would enable the customer to conceal the flaw. No one ever complained, as they were so pleased to have been able to buy a carpet.

The main trade in those days was infact linoleum. Very shortly, however, carpets became more plentiful and the age of wall-to-wall carpet began. Here the firm was at a disadvantage because of the size of the shop. The small premises meant that not many rolls of carpet could be stocked.

Fortunately, as one door closed another opened. Fylde Floors pioneered the sale of lino tiles in Blackpool. They literally stocked thousands and set up an excellent and profitable side to the business.

In 1959 the company was offered a lease on part of the corner unit where the business is located today. This enabled it to carry larger stocks of 27-inch body carpet and establish connections with leading manufacturers.

When Wilfred retired Alfred's late brother Billy joined the business along with another company stalwart, the late Michael Cretney. Now there were two shops next to each other, though separated by a small thoroughfare, one stocking linoleum and tiles, and the other carpets.

Early in the 1960s the remainder of the original site, two shops and six flats, was acquired. The whole ground floor was turned into shop and office space. In the 1970s another part of the corner was taken, followed by an expansion which included premises in Bispham. Alfred's brother Billy took on the running of the Bispham site, which subsequently became a wholly separate business.

The 1970s saw the advent of broadloom carpet, and a steady decline in the sale of 27-inch body carpet which was soon phased out. In 1979 Alfred's youngest son Jeremy joined the business. The company took on a different unit in Bispham again in 1988, with Alfred's eldest son Andrew joining the business. During this time the business changed again, with less emphasis on having large stocks of carpet and more on selling from manufacturers' patterns and displays, giving the customer a wider choice than ever. The sale in patterned carpets declined as plains and naturals became fashionable.

The company now expanded into the contract carpeting business; meanwhile the renovation of the upstairs corner unit was followed by the addition of a beds and bedroom furniture section.

Above left: *The late Les Dawson pays a vist to Fylde Floor Company in the mid-1980s.* ***Below:*** *Brothers Jeremy and Andrew Shillito in the Blackpool showroom.*

Fox Brothers - Efficiency and Reliability

Fox Brothers Ltd is one of the area's best known names in the world of haulage and plant-hire. Since the 1930s when the family firm was founded it has grown in size, status and reputation. Throughout those years it has remained true to the ethos of efficiency and reliability first set by its founders eight decades ago.

In was in 1932 that the name of Fox Brothers was first established on the Fylde Coast. Over the years that followed three generations of brothers have worked hard to build up what is now a group of companies from a single-faceted haulage company into the well established enterprise that exists today.

Two farming brothers, Jack and Clarence Fox, started the firm with a single passenger coach and one wagon based in Blackpool's Garstang Road.

The 1930s – the 'hungry thirties' were in fact the most difficult decade of the twentieth century in which to start a business. Unemployment soared into the millions, the economic downturn was unprecedented, a downturn which would last until the outbreak of the Second World War in 1939. Businesses were closing at record levels.

Yet armed with unlimited enthusiasm, eagerness to achieve something with their lives, and a huge capacity for hard work the two Fox brothers swam against the prevailing current.

Before long the fledgling firm was employing up to 15 staff and able to buy new wagons at the then high price of £1,000.

Above left: Demolition work at Blackpool Tower. ***Below:*** Putting a Fox Brothers crane to work. ***Bottom:*** A Fox Brothers cab and trailer.

Inevitably when war broke out new problems had to be faced. Men who had worked for the firm were called up to join the armed forces, fuel was in short supply and new vehicles impossible to obtain. The brothers tried hard to provide support for their men's families whilst they were away. And if there were problems there were also new opportunities - war work with haulage contracts for defence contracts which would not otherwise have existed.

At war's end in 1945 many predicted another economic crash. The late 1940s would indeed prove difficult years. Yet those firms which did survive those austere times into the 1950s and 1960s were able to reap the benefits of a rapidly growing economy.

Jack Fox's son, Harold 'Barney' Fox, joined the business. Jack and Harold, ably assisted by right hand men John Flatters and Eddy Parker, would drive the firm forward to become much more than a simple haulage business.

The firm became a limited company in 1954, a change which provided the base to fine-tune and strengthen the business in order to be able to offer both private and corporate customers a whole range of lifting, excavation and haulage services using any one of more than fifty items of plant. From simply being a haulage company clients are now offered such items as mobile cranes, tower cranes, road sweepers and concrete wagons – not to mention trained drivers to operate the company's equipment or those of the clients.

Most work today is in the North West of England, but staff inevitably find themselves not only working all over the United Kingdom but also sometimes further afield in Europe.

Down the years the firm moved from its original base in Garstang Road to Wakefield Road, Bispham. It later moved to Holyoake Avenue, Bispham, before finally relocating to its present base at Holly Road on the Redmarsh industrial estate at Thornton, just north of Blackpool.

Fox Brothers Ltd of the 21st century bears little outward resemblance to the business founded in the 1930s. From just two vehicles costing a thousand pounds or less, dozens of vehicles and specialised plant costing more than £100,000 each are now available for use. Staff numbers have grown from just two to approaching fifty. Yet, despite those vast changes, the business still operates using the same business ethics that prevailed when Jack and Clarence Fox first set up the family firm – a commitment to honest service, reliability, courtesy and, above all, pride in the job.

It is those values, along with the expertise and experience of everyone at Fox Brothers that has brought the company the status it now enjoys.

Today the brothers at Fox Brothers Ltd are Harold Fox's sons, Alan and Robert, with a fourth generation of the family, in the shape of their nephew and Harold's grandson Paul Fox, having now joined the family firm.

*Above: A Fox Brothers 16-ton excavator. **Below:** One of the company's Terex PPM 600 mobile cranes.*

Lyndene Hotel - Lighting up the Promenade

Millions of folk come and visit Blackpool every year. Some come just for the day; many stay just for a weekend, others enjoy the local delights for a week or more. Since the birth of this iconic seaside resort the demand for accommodation has never slackened. And in the wake of that demand the accommodation for visitors has grown, expanded and evolved for over a century.

Few towns can have been blessed with such a variety of places to stay – from the most expensive of luxury hotels to the humblest of boarding houses.

Famously some families enjoyed their stay in Blackpool so much that, year after year, they would book their next year's holiday at they same boarding house on the last day of their holidays.

That kind of loyalty is rare these days. Yet today, in the 21st century, at least one Blackpool hotel still manages to please its guests so much that they do still come back again and again and again.

The Lyndene Hotel is one of Blackpool's largest family-owned and run hotels, it offers 21st century standards, alongside the friendliest of welcomes. Open all year, the hotel is situated in a superb Promenade position, between Central and South Pier, themselves between the Tower and the Pleasure Beach, providing an ideal base for holidays and breaks.

The Hotel offers over 140 fully equipped and tastefully decorated en suite bedrooms, enhanced with wall-mounted flat screen LCD televisions with Freeview/Radio, in room safes, hospitality trays, hairdryers and telephones. Three lifts provide access to all three floors plus there is a selection of ground floor rooms. Smoking bedrooms are available.

With three licensed bars and two magnificent air-conditioned, sea view cabaret lounges, the Lyndene Hotel offers quality compered entertainment every night of the year, from fabulous vocalists to side-splitting comedians. There is also a superb keyboard player, playing most afternoons and early evenings.

Known for the high standard and varied choice of cuisine, dining is a pleasure in either of the two quality restaurants. A variety of all day snacks and light refreshments are available in one of the sea view bar lounges, where guests can enjoy the panoramic views of the Irish Sea and Promenade.

Top: A Lyndene brochure from the 1980s, prior to expansion. Below left: Receiving a warm and friendly welcome from the reception staff. Below: The hotel's restaurant and dining area.

Working seven days a week, 365 days a year, being personally involved not only as hosts but also as, cleaners, porters, cooks, waiters and bar staff, Barry and Carole's unique brand of hard work and friendliness soon paid dividends.

In 1993, now joined by daughter Deborah and son in law Steven Dunn, a major expansion programme was put into action. From the hotel's original 33 rooms the building was massively expanded and rebuilt to provide not only 140 bedrooms but also a new standard for Blackpool hotels.

Owners are Barry and Carole Young. The husband and wife team of hoteliers took on the Lyndene in 1985, though by then they were already seasoned Blackpool veterans.

Barry and Carole's first venture in catering for Blackpool's tourist trade came in 1977 when they took on the challenge of running Holman House, a small hotel, in Lytham Road. That was followed the next year by the 10 bedroom Katrina in Lonsdale Road, and two years after that by the 14 bedroom Derby House Hotel in Tydsley Road.

In June 1985 came the biggest challenge yet when Barry and Carole found what they had really been looking for all along. At that time the Lyndene, perfectly located on the promenade, boasted just 33 rooms, but there was room to accommodate not only guests but also Barry and Carole's ambitious plans for the hotel's future.

Nothing of course can be achieved without hard effort. According to Barry and Carole, if they had known in 1978 what difficulties would lie ahead of them they might never have begun the remarkable journey which has led to today's Lyndene Hotel. Yet it has all been worth it: Barry and Carole say they love their work and meeting their guests so much that they are planning not to retire but to carry on forever.

And are their guests equally pleased? You bet they are: an inspection of the hotel Guest Book quickly reveals what they think: "Fabulous: we've already booked again for next year".

Above: Fun and games of an evening 365 nights of the year.
Below: The impressive Lyndene Hotel facia by night.

Banks Carrington & Co.

Providing Blackpool with a Personal Service since 1881

Specialising in residential and commercial conveyancing, as well as probate, wills and trusts, the legal firm of Banks Carrington & Co., based in Edward Street, is one of the best known in Blackpool.

In 1879 William Banks, a prominent Preston solicitor, had a branch office at 10, Church Street, Blackpool. By 1887 he had moved to 33, Church Street, and later, in 1892, to 45, Church Street.

Despite very small beginnings the office prospered. Many important businessmen involved in Blackpool's development became clients. At the same time, whilst looking after the needs of these developers and entrepreneurs, the firm attended to the needs of the

ordinary public: the landau drivers, the pleasure boat and bathing van attendants, the smallholders and the many hoteliers and boarding house proprietors.

William Banks died in 1893 and, by 1896, the firm of W. Banks & Company, now under the stewardship of Edward Charles Banks and John Underhill, had moved to 16, Birley Street.

Not long afterwards, Harry Cartmell, a former assistant of William Banks, took over the running of the Blackpool office. Through three generations the Cartmell family would continue to look after the legal needs of the Blackpool and Fylde coast population. Harry Cartmell, later to become Sir Harry, shared his time between the Blackpool and Preston offices combining these activities with the duties of being Mayor of Preston between 1914 and 1917.

The firm moved to its present premises in 1931. Built in 1869, the building was originally guesthouse accommodation. Along with most others along Edward Street they were converted into offices in the 20th century.

Since the last member of the Cartmell family's retirement in 1984, Alan Carrington has been sole principal.

In the mid-1990s the firm changed its name, following the separation of the Blackpool and Preston offices. Under its new title, Banks Carrington & Co., it is still catering for the needs of Blackpool's business community as well as the everyday legal needs of ordinary folk.

The firm prides itself on providing a friendly and efficient service, offering home visits or out of hours appointments where necessary and being at all times available to everyone.

*Top: Sir Harry Cartmell during his term as Mayor. **Above left:** A certificate awarded to Sir Harry Cartmell on his election as Mayor from The Blackpool, Fleetwood and Fylde District Law Society. **Above:** Mr Alan Carrington with staff members Helen Thain (left), Barbara Simone (second from right) and Elaine Hallam (right).*

Ai Claims Solutions - Problem Solved

In the last decade Ai Claims Solutions has become one of Blackpool's most rapidly growing enterprises. Today the company occupies three buildings in the town: Indemnity House, Viscount Court and Atlantic House.

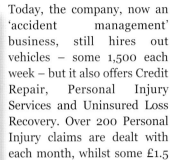

Viscount Court with its on-site restaurant facility was purpose built in 2005 for the expanding business.

Originally founded as the Four Lane Car Hire Company, Ai – short for Auto Indemnity - was formed in Blackpool in 1991.

Subsequently the firm moved to Bispham by which time the company had some 40 staff. By 2001 when Ai moved to Indemnity House there were 89 staff. Today some 375 staff work for Ai in Blackpool, 200 of whom work in the operations side of the call centre.

That growth has come through expansion and diversification. From simply providing hire cars for road traffic accident victims whilst their vehicles were being repaired, the firm has evolved into a business which handles every aspect of insurance claims arising from traffic accidents.

Providing an integrated service to both insurance providers and the insured means everyone is a winner: for insurers the costs of repair and replacement are minimised, whilst for the individual Ai's streamlined one-stop-shop approach means minimum fuss and maximum service.

Today, the company, now an 'accident management' business, still hires out vehicles – some 1,500 each week – but it also offers Credit Repair, Personal Injury Services and Uninsured Loss Recovery. Over 200 Personal Injury claims are dealt with each month, whilst some £1.5 million is recovered from insurers each week.

Through the company's operating arms – Ai Claims Solutions, Ai Repair Solutions, Ai Broker Solutions, Ai Automotive Solutions and Ai Fleet Solutions – the firm provides the kind of accident service that everyone would like to have.

Today, from its small beginnings in 1991, under Chairman Stephen Broughton and Chief Executive David Sandhu, Ai is a multi-million pound business quoted on the Stock Exchange.

Years of business innovation have propelled Ai into the forefront of its field.

And whilst cars continue to be driven, and accidents continue to happen, the future looks bright for this dynamic Blackpool business.

*Top left, left and below: Ai's Viscount Court, Indemnity House and Atlantic House premises. **Below:** Chairman, Stephen Broughton (left) and Chief Executive, David Sandhu, 2009.*

ACKNOWLEDGMENTS

The publishers would like to sincerely thank a number of individuals and organisations for their help and contribution to this publication.
This book would have been almost impossible without the kind co-operation of the following:

Local and Family History Centre at Blackpool Central Library

National Monuments Record (NMR), the public archive of English Heritage.
For further information about these images please telephone: 01793 414600
or email: nmrinfo@english-heritage.org.uk

Press Association Images

Bradford Industrial Museum

The Humphrey Spender Worktown Mass Observation Project
Copyright Bolton Council from the Bolton Museum Archive Service.